Mastering French Words

Level Up Your Vocabulary with Over 2500 French Words in Context

© **Copyright 2019**

All Rights Reserved. No part of this book may be reproduced in any form without permission in writing from the author. Reviewers may quote brief passages in reviews.

Disclaimer: No part of this publication may be reproduced or transmitted in any form or by any means, mechanical or electronic, including photocopying or recording, or by any information storage and retrieval system, or transmitted by email without permission in writing from the publisher.

While all attempts have been made to verify the information provided in this publication, neither the author nor the publisher assumes any responsibility for errors, omissions or contrary interpretations of the subject matter herein.

This book is for entertainment purposes only. The views expressed are those of the author alone, and should not be taken as expert instruction or commands. The reader is responsible for his or her own actions.

Adherence to all applicable laws and regulations, including international, federal, state and local laws governing professional licensing, business practices, advertising and all other aspects of doing business in the US, Canada, UK or any other jurisdiction is the sole responsibility of the purchaser or reader.

Neither the author nor the publisher assumes any responsibility or liability whatsoever on the behalf of the purchaser or reader of these materials. Any perceived slight of any individual or organization is purely unintentional.

Contents

INTRODUCTION 1

CHAPTER 1 – ARTICLES, PRONOUNS AND COMMON PREPOSITIONS 3

    SUBJECT/OBJECT PRONOUN: I, YOU, HE… 3

    POSSESSIVE ARTICLES: 5

    DEFINITE AND INDEFINITE ARTICLES: 7

    COMMON PREPOSITIONS: 8

    INTERROGATIVE PRONOUNS: 9

CHAPTER 2 – COMMON ADJECTIVES 10

    COLORS: 10

    DESCRIBING PEOPLE: 10

    DESCRIBING ITEMS: 20

    DESCRIBING A PERFORMANCE, A WORK: 21

CHAPTER 3 – TIME AND SPACE 23

    TIME: 23

    WEATHER: 30

    PLACE: 31

Prepositions – where is this? 35
Moving around and being somewhere: 36
Place – verbs of movement: 38

CHAPTER 4 – COMMON ADVERBS 40
Adverbs relating to quantity: 40
Adverbs relating to quality: 41
Adverbs and conjunctions related to time: 42

CHAPTER 5 – HOUSES AND LODGINGS 45
Electrical appliances: 51

CHAPTER 6 – COMMON FRENCH VERBS: AN OVERVIEW 52

CHAPTER 7 – BUYING THINGS AND PAYING 88

CHAPTER 8 – NUMBERS AND THE HOUR 92
Numbers: 92
Tell the hour: 95

CHAPTER 9 – ARGUING: COMMON VERBS AND NOUNS 97
Structuring your argument and explaining cause and consequence: 99

CHAPTER 10 – INFORMAL SPEECH / INTERJECTIONS 104

CHAPTER 11 – MEETING SOMEONE 108
For the first time: 108
Asking more questions: 109
Keeping in touch: 111
Asking for updates: 112

CHAPTER 12 – SCHEDULING A GET-TOGETHER: 114
In town – at the local theater / cinema: 114
In town – eating out: 115
About scheduling a meet-up: 117

CHAPTER 13 – TRAVELING: 119
Being on the way: 119
Trips and holidays: 121

THINGS TO DO: 123
NATURE AND LANDSCAPES: 124
CONCLUSION: **126**

Introduction

Being able to express yourself in a new language can often seem like a daunting task: you might be able to understand what the other person is saying, but then finding the right words on your own is a completely different challenge. That's why we've developed this book: it not only inventories common vocabulary that you may need on a daily basis (meeting new people, talking about where you're going, or describing what you like doing), but also offers synonyms and related expressions that will enable you to talk about things from different angles. For instance, you'll know about how to describe somebody's behavior, but you'll also learn common French expressions about it, which you normally wouldn't see in most textbooks. Another section is dedicated to common interjections in oral speech, which you may have already heard, but not identified – they'll be crystal clear now! A good portion of this book is also dedicated to the most common French verbs you'll find: they'll help you refine your thoughts and gradually expand the range of topics you can talk and think about.

This book is mostly aimed at boosting your vocabulary to help you create natural sounding sentences; it is therefore recommended that you learn the basics of French (pronunciation, important articles, placement of adjectives, common verb conjugations) before using this book. This book is centered around improving your expression and the quality of your speaking and writing across different registers. Being able to review vocabulary centered around a particular theme is especially powerful when building connections between the new words. We've also largely focused on immediately usable words, adjectives, and adverbs that you can easily integrate into your sentences and perfect as you go.

You'll also find sentence examples for you to see in real time how French is spoken and said: we've mostly stressed this point in our giant "verb bank", where you'll start crafting stronger sentences, getting your thoughts out more clearly, and get a solid grasp of French syntax.

Note: all adjectives will be presented with their masculine and feminine forms in the singular. Unless plural forms are irregular (as opposed to the most common form, which is when an "s" gets added to the masculine and feminine version of the adjective), we generally won't indicate it.

Chapter 1 – Articles, Pronouns and Common Prepositions

Subject/Object pronoun: I, you, he…

- I – *je*

- you (singular, informal) – *tu*

- he – *il*

- she – *elle*

- it – *il, elle* (depending on the object's gender); *c'* (when referring to an event, a concept)

> It (the book) was fantastic – *Il (le livre) était fantastique.*

> It's crazy (talking about a fair – *une fête*)! – *C'est fou !*

- we – *nous*

- you (plural; singular, formal) – *vous*

> What would you like for dinner, ma'am? – *Qu'est-ce que vous aimeriez pour le dîner, madame ?*

> Listen to me, all of you! – *Ecoutez-moi bien, vous tous !*

- they – *ils, elles* (if there is as much as one male person or male item in the whole group, then the article will switch to *ils*)

> They (my aunt and my uncle) went to South Africa last week – *Ils sont allés en Afrique du Sud la semaine dernière.*

> They (my two sisters) really like this rock band – *Elles aiment vraiment ce groupe de rock.*

We will now introduce you to indirect pronouns in French, which can be constructed in two different ways, just as in English – the other variant is that pronouns change in French depending on the syntax:

> I gave him an apple – *Je lui ai donné une pomme.*

> >>> *ai donné*: passé composé (compound past tense) of the verb *donner* (to give), plus common auxiliary *avoir* conjugated in the present and first-person singular – *j'ai*.

> >>> him: appended before the verb in a construction quite similar to English – *lui*.

> I gave an apple to him – *J'ai donné une pomme à lui* (the construction for the verb *donner* is in itself unnatural, but it gives you a better idea of what can happen in French.)

Let us take *to belong*, for instance, which uses *to* in English and requires a pronoun introduced with *à* in French:

> The cat belongs to me – *Le chat m'appartient. / Le chat appartient à moi.*

In French, both the structures you can see above work fluently: it serves to highlight how most of the usual pronouns will change from one to the other, and so will the syntax.

- to me – *à moi* / me *(m'* if followed by a vowel)

> It's to me that David gave the magazine – *C'est à moi que David a donné le magazine.*

> He took my toy – *Il m'a pris mon jouet.*

- to you (singular, informal) – *à toi / te (t')*

> I'll send you a postcard once I get there – *Je t'enverrai une carte postale dès que j'arrive là-bas.*
>
> It's yours – *C'est à toi.*

- to him – *à lui / lui*

> What should I buy him? – *Qu'est-ce que je devrais lui acheter ?*

- to her – *à elle / lui*

> Give her your hand – *Donne-lui ta main.*
>
> Why didn't you give the dress to her? – *Pourquoi est-ce que ce n'est pas à elle que tu as donné la robe ?*

- to it – *à lui, à elle* (depending on the gender) / *lui*
- to us – *à nous / nous*
- to you – *à vous / vous*
- to them – *à eux / leur*

> I suggested to them to buy it instead – *Je leur ai suggéré de l'acheter plutôt.*

Well, ask them! – *Et bien demande-leur !*

Possessive articles:

There are two major differences between English and French:

- possessive articles change gender depending on the object they are attached to (my aunt, *ma tante*; my uncle, *mon oncle*)

- when you get to "his" and "her", it will equally be the object in question that will determine the article: you won't know the possessor's gender from looking at the article.

You'll have the singular masculine *(m)* and feminine *(f)* versions for each article, as well as its plural form. The article remains the same in the plural, no matter the noun's gender.

- my – *mon, ma, mes*

    My computer is broken – *Mon ordinateur (m) est cassé.*

My wrists are blue, see? – *Mes poignets (m) sont bleus, tu vois ?*

- your (singular, informal) – *ton, ta, tes*

    Did you forget your glasses at the beach? – *As-tu oublié tes lunettes (f) à la plage ?*

    Your sister is coming to see us this weekend – *Ta soeur (f) vient nous voir ce week-end.*

- his – *son, sa, ses*

    You should ask him if you can borrow his phone to make a call – *Tu devrais lui demander si tu peux lui emprunter son téléphone pour passer un appel.*

    >>> to make a call – *passer un appel*

- her – *son, sa, ses*

    I want to know where she got her shoes – *Je veux savoir où elle a trouvé ses (f) chaussures.*

- its – *son, sa, ses*

    Its software is the best on the market – *Ses (m) logiciels sont les meilleurs du marché.*

    >>> a software – *un logiciel* (generally, "software" on its own tends to be in the plural in French)

- our – *notre, notre, nos*

    Our new house should be built by the end of next month – *Notre nouvelle maison (f) devrait être construite d'ici la fin du mois prochain / d'ici la fin du mois* or *à la fin du mois* (not both)

- your – *votre, votre, vos*

> Don't forget your coats when you leave – *N'oubliez pas vos manteaux (m) quand vous partez.*

- their – *leur, leur, leurs*

> They're really good at their respective jobs – *Ils sont très bons à leur travail (m) respectif.*

> >>> Whereas English prefers to put "jobs" in the plural here because there are several jobs overall, French puts it in the singular to single out each person's job.

> I met their mutual friend yesterday – *J'ai rencontré leur ami commun hier.*

> >>> mutual – *mutuel, commun*

Definite and indefinite articles:

- the – *le, la, les* (masculine singular, feminine singular, plural in either gender)

> I brought the kids back home – *J'ai ramené les enfants à la maison.*

> The glasses are in the sink – *Les verres sont dans l'évier.*

- no article in the plural – *des*

> Wolves passed us by as we were hiking in the woods – *Des loups nous sont passés devant pendant que nous étions en train de faire une randonnée dans la forêt.*

> >>> to hike – *faire une randonnée*

- a – *un, une* (masculine singular, feminine singular)

> He crumpled a newspaper and tossed it in the bin – *Il chiffonna un journal et le lança dans la poubelle.*

> >>> to crumple – *chiffonner, froisser*

> >>> a bin – *une poubelle*

- this (as an article) – *ce*

    I think this movie is overrated – *Je trouve que ce film est surfait.*

- that (as an article) – *ce*

    That wallpaper surprised me when I first saw it – *Ce papier peint m'a surpris quand je l'ai vu pour la première fois.*

- this (as a pronoun) – *ça*

    I like this – *J'aime ça.*

- that (as a pronoun) – *ça*

    I found that a bit terrifying – *J'ai trouvé ça assez terrifiant.*

Common prepositions:

- of (a part of) – *de, du (de+le), de la, de l'* (*de* + masculine / feminine word starting with a vowel or an 'h'), *des*

    I brought you a slice of pie since I know how much you like them – *Je t'ai apporté une part de gâteau comme je sais à quel point tu aimes ça.*

    Calculus will be a part of your curriculum – *L'algèbre fera partie de votre programme / curriculum.*

    She's always been afraid of spiders – *Elle a toujours eu peur des araignées.*

He's coming back from the hospital today – *Il revient de l'hôpital (m) aujourd'hui.*

    A part of the old church collapsed during the night – *Une partie de la vieille église s'est effondrée pendant la nuit.*

- from – *de, du, de la, de l', des*

    I come from France – *Je viens de France.*

    They travelled from England to the US – *Ils ont voyagé d'Angleterre jusqu'aux Etats-Unis.*

She's returning from the Azores on Friday – *Elle revient des Açores vendredi.*

- at – *à* and its compounds: *au, à la, à l', aux*

   I need to go to the emergency room – *Je dois aller aux urgences* (*les urgences* is always plural in French).

   I need to go to the pharmacy – *Je dois aller à la pharmacie.*

Interrogative pronouns:

- What? (alone) – *Quoi ?*
- What …? – *Qu'est-ce que… ?*

   What happened? – *Qu'est-ce qu'il s'est passé ?*
- Who? – *Qui ?*

   Who is this person? – *Qui est cette personne ?*
- Where? – *Où ?*

   Where do you live? – *Où habites-tu ?*
- When? – *Quand ?*

   When should we meet? – *Quand devrions-nous nous voir ?*

Chapter 2 – Common Adjectives

Colors:

- blue – *bleu(e)*

- green – *vert(e)*

- yellow – *jaune*

- orange – *orange*

- red – *rouge*

- pink – *rose*

- purple – *violet, violette*

- grey – *gris, grise*

- brown – *marron*

- black – *noir(e)*

- white – *blanc, blanche*

Describing people:

- tall – *grand(e)*

- small – *petit(e)*

- big – *gros, grosse*

- thin – *maigre, fin(e)*

>I found him really thin – *Je l'ai trouvé vraiment maigre.*

- old – *vieux, vieille*

- young – *jeune*

- wrinkled – *ridé, ridée*

- nice – *gentil, gentille*

- altruistic – *altruiste* (both genders)

- generous – *généreux, généreuse*

>>>> Pay attention to the following French expression which can have two meanings:

Il a le coeur sur la main – He's always willing to give to others. (most common meaning)

Il a le cœur sur la main – He wears his heart on his sleeve.

- pessimistic – *pessimiste*

>You shouldn't be so pessimistic, and instead work on your flaws – *Tu ne devrais pas être aussi pessimiste, et plutôt travailler sur tes défauts / chercher à corriger tes défauts.*

>>>> *chercher à corriger*, literally "Seek to correct…"

- optimistic – *optimiste*

>Keeping an optimistic outlook on life will get him far – *Le fait qu'il garde un point de vue optimiste sur la vie l'emmènera loin.* ("The fact that he guards an optimistic outlook…", literally; sentences starting with: "Doing…" in English are either translated as *Le fait que* + subject + verb, or *que* + subject + verb [more formal])

- hopeful – *optimiste*, but hopefully – *heureusement* (adverb), subject + *espérer* (conjugated) + *que*...

I'm hopeful things will get better – *J'espère que tout ira mieux.*

>>> things go well – *ça va bien / ça va mieux ; tout va bien / tout va mieux.*

- lousy (he's a lousy dancer) – *c'est un (très) mauvais danseur*

He's no artist – *il n'a rien d'un artiste.*

- skillful – *doué(e)*

- good (he's/she's pretty good) – *bon, bonne ; il est plutôt bon / elle est plutôt bonne*

- to be good (at painting, drawing, glassblowing) – *être bon en peinture, en dessin, en soufflage de verre* or *être bon peintre, dessinateur/trice, souffleur/euse de verre*

- to be good (at football, …) – *être bon en foot*

He's a good guy – *C'est un bon gars.*

- clumsy – *maladroit*

> His introduction was a bit clumsy, but hopefully it was intelligible – *Son introduction était un petit peu maladroite, mais heureusement elle était compréhensible.*
>
> Being clumsy, I'd rather not have any breakable objects around the house – *Comme je suis maladroit(e), je préférerais ne pas avoir d'objets cassables dans la maison.*

- polite – *poli(e)*

- courteous – *courtois(e)*

> Our hosts were very courteous – *Nos hôtes étaient très polis.*

- rude; disrespectful – *malpoli(e) ; irrespectueux, -se*

- well-behaved – *bien éduqué(e), bien élevé(e)* (mostly for children)

What a well-behaved child, I'm impressed! – *Quel enfant bien élevé, je suis impressionné !*

- have good manners – *avoir de bonnes manières, bien se comporter*

I find it particularly important to have good manners – *Je trouve qu'il est particulièrement important d'avoir de bonnes manières / de bien se comporter.*

- doubtful – pronoun + *douter* + que + verb in the subjunctive present

I'm doubtful it'll work – *Je doute que ça marche.*

- uncertain – *incertain(e)*

- unsure – *pas sûr(e)*

- unsure of oneself – *ne pas être sûr(e) de soi* (*de moi*, "of myself", *de toi*, "of yourself"…)

He's unsure of himself – *Il n'est pas sûr de lui.*

- wary (of people, experiences) – subject + *se méfier de* + noun / verb

I'm wary of meeting new people – *Je me méfie de rencontrer de nouvelles personnes.*

- silent – *silencieux, silencieuse*

He remained silent – *Il demeura / resta silencieux.*

>>> to keep / be silent may also be translated as *être muré dans le silence* (He kept silent for days – *Il fut muré dans le silence pendant des jours.*)

- alone – *seul, seule*

- lonely – *solitaire* (both genders), *se sentir seul(e)* ; may also be *être seul*, (although less so because it may be confused with "alone")

While I like being alone, I never feel lonely – *Même si j'aime être seul(e), je ne me sens jamais seul.*

He always keeps to himself – *Il est toujours renfermé (sur lui-même).*

She likes going for walks on her own – *Elle aime se balader toute seule / en solitaire.*

> They're lone wolves, there's nothing wrong with that – *Ce sont des loups solitaires, il n'y a rien de mal à ça.*

- bubbly – *pétillant(e), pétillants, pétillantes*
- charming – *charmant(e), charmants, charmantes*

> Perhaps we should hire someone who's more bubbly and charming as a receptionist? – *Peut-être que nous devrions engager quelqu'un qui soit plus pétillant et charmant en tant que réceptionniste ?*

- approachable – *accessible, ouvert(e)*

She's always approachable – *Elle est toujours accessible / ouverte.*

- ambitious – *ambitieux, -se*

> All the contestants were quite ambitious this year – *Tous les participants étaient assez ambitieux cette année.*

- competitive – *compétitif, -ve*
- confident in oneself – *confiant, -e en soi (en moi, "*in myself*", en toi, "*in yourself*"…)*
- self-assured – *sûr de soi*

> As he stepped onto the stage, I noticed how self-assured he was – *Alors qu'il montait sur l'estrade, je remarquai à quel point il était sûr de lui.*

- to have an unwavering confidence – *avoir toujours confiance en soi / être confiant* (but never: *être + soi*)

> He has an unwavering confidence even when everything seems impossible – *Il est toujours confiant / Il a toujours*

confiance en lui / ne perd jamais confiance en lui, même quand tout semble impossible.

- to lack confidence – *manquer de confiance en soi*

- to have low self-esteem – *ne pas avoir confiance en soi* (commonly used), *ne pas avoir confiance en soi-même* (this option is the most common)

> Although he has low-esteem, he is always doing something and trying new hobbies – *Même s'il n'a pas confiance en lui, il est toujours en train de faire quelque chose et d'essayer de nouveaux hobbies.*
>
> \>>> It may also be translated as *ne pas avoir d'estime de soi* (or *Il n'a pas d'estime de soi,* literally "He does not have self-esteem", although it is often derogatory and judgmental).

- overwhelmed – *dépassé(e)*

He always looks overwhelmed – *Il a toujours l'air dépassé.*

- disheartened – *dépité(e)*

- boastful, pedantic – *pédant* (generally only male); *vantard(e)*

As boastful as he may be… – *Aussi pédant / vantard qu'il puisse être…*

> I doubt she'll stop boasting about her accomplishments – *Je doute qu'elle arrête de se vanter / de vanter ses accomplissements.*

- prideful – *fier, -ère*

- to have pride in one's work, accomplishments – *être fier de son travail, de ses accomplissements*

- frail, weak – *fragile*

- weak-willed – *avoir peu de volonté, être sans volonté*

- strong – *fort(e)*

- aggressive – *agressif, -ve*

- bossy, authoritarian – *autoritaire*

    They fired her colleague because she was too bossy around all other employees – *Ils ont licencié sa collègue parce qu'elle était trop autoritaire autour de tous les autres employés.*

- egotistical, selfish – *égoïste* (both genders)
- fussy – *irritable ; pointilleux, pointilleuse*

    The biggest downside when working with fussy colleagues is that every tiny mistake is open to scrutiny – *Le plus gros inconvénient quand on travaille avec des collègues pointilleux est que chaque minuscule erreur est passée au crible.*

    >>> *passer au crible*, idiom: criticize virulently or repeatedly.

- (im)patient – *(im)patiente, -e*

    My boss is always impatient around deadlines – *Mon boss est toujours impatient quand on s'approche des délais / de la fin des délais.*

    >>> *délais* is the period of time between the start and the end of a project, not only the end – *quand on s'approche des délais* is literally "When we get closer to deadlines."

Expressions related to failure:

- to be a sore loser – *être un mauvais perdant*
- to take failure in stride – *bien se remettre de ses échecs* ("To recover well from one's failures")

    I admire him because he always takes failures in stride and keeps working – *Je l'admire parce qu'il se remet toujours de ses échecs et continue de travailler.*

- There's no use crying over spilt milk – *ça ne sert à rien de pleurer sur ce qui a été fait*

- Looking back won't help you – *Regarder en arrière ne va pas t'aider.*

- to get back into the saddle – *remonter en selle*

Don't worry, I'll get back into the saddle – *Ne t'inquiète pas, je remontrai en selle.*

- wealthy, rich – *riche*

> He's a particularly rich man – *C'est un homme particulièrement riche.*

- poor – *pauvre*

- a pauper – *un pauvre*

- homeless – *sans-abri*, SDF (abbreviation for *Sans Domicile Fixe*, "Without fixed abode")

- pretty; handsome – *beau, belle, beaux, belles* (*beau* here compounds both the English adjectives, and so can be used for people of both genders)

- well-kept (of someone's appearance) – *soigné(e)*

> One could hardly be any more well-kept: even her fingernails have been trimmed down to the last millimeter – *On pourrait difficilement être plus soigné : même ses ongles ont été limés au millimètre près.* (*au millimètre / centimètre / mètre près*: [down] to the last …)

- unkempt, disheveled – *négligé* (*avoir l'air négligé, une apparence négligée*), *en bataille* (*avoir les cheveux en bataille*, "to have disheveled hair")

> What I mean is that he would still be unkempt even without disheveled hair – *Ce que je veux dire, c'est qu'il aurait toujours l'air négligé même sans les cheveux de bataille.*

- smart (well-dressed) – *bien habillé(e), élégant(e), chic* (both genders)

He may look smart in his new attire, but we all know he's not that smart at all – *Il a peut-être l'air élégant / chic dans son nouvel ensemble, mais nous savons tous qu'il n'est pas si intelligent que ça.*

- smart (intelligent) – *intelligent(e)*
- analytical – *analytique*
- tired – *fatigué(e)*

Would you excuse me, I feel quite tired – *Veuillez m'excuser, je me sens un peu / quelque peu* (formal) *fatigué(e).*

>>> related: tirelessly – *sans relâche* (idiom: literally "Without loosening, relaxing"); *sans en démordre* (idiom: literally "Without unbiting", as though you were fully immersed in something and wouldn't / couldn't let go before finishing your work).

We've all worked tirelessly today: here's some snacks! – *Nous avons tous travaillé sans relâche aujourd'hui : voici quelques snacks / friandises !*

- exhausted – *éreinté(e)*

I'm exhausted from hiking – *Je suis éreinté à cause de la randonnée* (a *randonnée* is a hike in French; literally "I'm exhausted because of the hike").

- weary – *las, lasse ; fatigué(e)*

He barely noticed us as he was weary from work – *Il nous remarqua à peine, comme il était fatigué à cause du travail.*

- drowsy – *somnolent(e) ; fatigué(e),* this is more common, may replace it in oral speech

He suddenly told us he felt drowsy, then went to bed upstairs – *Soudain, il nous dit qu'il se sentait somnolent / fatigué, puis il monta se coucher*

>>> We'll have the occasion to review how French creates movement verbs in Chapter 3; for now, take note of this construction. Here, *monter* means "to go upstairs", and *se coucher* is a common pronominal verb meaning "to go to bed".

- He sleeps like a log – *Il dort comme un loir.*

- insomniac – *insomniaque*

- to have insomnia – *avoir des insomnies, souffrir d'insomnies* (always in the plural in these expressions)

> I went outside to drink some tea because I have insomnia – *Je suis allé boire du thé dehors parce que je souffre d'insomnies.*

- be hungry – *avoir faim*

I'm so hungry I could eat a horse! – *J'ai une faim de loup !* (idiom: "I have a wolf's hunger")

I was so hungry – *J'avais tellement faim.*

- be starving – *être affamé(e)*

What are we eating tonight? I'm starving! – *Qu'est-ce qu'on mange ce soir ? Je suis affamé !*

- be thirsty – *avoir soif*

- crave, have cravings (food) – *avoir terriblement envie de...*

I'm craving strawberries right now! – *J'ai terriblement envie de fraises tout de suite !*

- surprised – *surpris(e)*

- amazed – *étonné(e), stupéfait(e)*

- shocked – *choqué(e)*

> He was shocked to learn about his reelection – *Il a été choqué d'apprendre sa réélection.*

- be dumbfounded by... - *être sans voix devant ...*

> I was dumbfounded by the amount of work they had put in! – *J'étais sans voix devant la quantité* ("amount") *de travail qu'ils avaient fournie ! (fournir ... – to give, put in)*

- be nonplussed by... – *être désarçonné par...*

Describing items:

- heavy – *lourd(e)*

> Be careful with this cardboard box, it's pretty heavy – *Fais attention avec cette boîte de carton, elle est plutôt lourde.*

- light – *léger, légère*

- fragile – *fragile*

- small – *petit(e)*

- huge – *énorme*

- broken – *cassé(e)*

- smashed – *fracassé(e)*

The picture had been smashed against a wall – *L'image avait été fracassée contre un mur.*

- smashed to pieces – *réduit en morceaux*

- shattered – *brisé(e), éclaté(e)*. Unless somebody explicitly does the shattering, French will prefer pronominal verbs, i.e. *se briser, s'éclater* conjugated in various tenses.

> My favorite glass shattered during our move – *Mon verre favori s'est brisé pendant notre déménagement.* (no one caused that in particular)

> He shattered the mirror – *Il a brisé le miroir.*

- in good shape – *en bon état*

- new – *nouveau, nouvelle*

- brand new – *tout nouveau, toute nouvelle*

    Did you hear? They've just launched a brand new smartphone yesterday! – *Tu as entendu ? Ils viennent juste de lancer un tout nouveau smartphone hier !*

- pristine – *intact(e)* ("not broken") ; *en parfait état* ("not broken" or "perfectly clean")

    I was surprised to see the crockery was pristine! – *J'étais surpris de voir que la vaisselle était intacte / en parfait état !*

- used, second-hand – *d'occasion* (after the noun)

I bought a pair of second-hand headphones – *J'ai acheté une paire d'écouteurs d'occasion.*

- old – *vieux, vieille*

    My nephew never cared for all these old books – *Mon neveu ne s'est jamais préoccupé de ces vieux livres.*

- elegant (jewelry, clothes) – *élégant(e)*

- classy - *élégant(e), chic* (both genders)

- stylish – *stylé(e)*

That was such a stylish interior – *C'était un intérieur tellement stylé !*

- hideous – *hideux, -se*

These curtains are hideous! – *Ces rideaux sont hideux !*

- unpleasant + noun – *ne pas plaire* ; see the following:

I found that decoration unpleasant – *Cette décoration ne me plaisait pas.*

Describing a performance, a work:

- a draft – *un brouillon*
- finished – *fini(e)*

- fleshed out – *précis(e)*

    The plan is a bit more fleshed out now – *Le plan est un peu plus précis maintenant.*

- perfect – *parfait(e)*
- marvelous – *merveilleux, -se*
- impressive – *impressionnant(e)*
- surprising – *surprenant(e)*
- lacking – *insuffisant(e)*

    We had good hopes for this project, but the final product was very lacking – *Nous avions de bons espoirs pour ce projet, mais le produit fini était très insuffisant.*

- mediocre – *médiocre, moyen(ne)*
- normal – *normal(e)*
- half-baked – *à moitié fini*

    You're not expecting me to accept this half-baked conclusion as your finished project? – *Tu ne t'attends quand même pas à ce que j'accepte cette conclusion à moitié finie comme étant ton projet terminé ?*

Chapter 3 – Time and Space

Time:

- a morning – *un matin, une matinée* (*matin* will be the word you'll predominantly use; matinée, on the other hand, is only used when describing how a particular morning is going: see *soirée, journée, année* below for such examples:)

We woke up early this morning – *Nous nous sommes réveillés tôt ce matin.*

It was a particularly snowy morning – *C'était une matinée particulièrement enneigée.*

- 9 AM – *neuf heures (du matin)*
- noon – *midi*
- an afternoon – *un / une après-midi* (both genders are commonly admitted in French)
- an evening – *un soir, une soirée* (*soirée* is now only used when describing the weather or the atmosphere of a particular evening;

when you want to refer to the time of the day, i.e. "We're in the evening and not in the morning", use *soir*)

- a night – *une nuit* (note: staying for one or only a couple of nights in an accommodation is often called *une nuitée / des nuitées*; contrary to *matinée* or *soirée*, here *nuitée* is solely used in that context)

- midnight – *minuit*

- during the day – *la journée*

- at night – *la nuit*

> He frequently wakes up at night and grabs something in the fridge – *Il se réveille fréquemment la nuit et prend quelque chose dans le réfrigérateur / le frigo.*

- a day – *un jour, une journée* (*journée* is only used in emphatic sentences when you talk about the weather, be it good or bad, or when talking about a day retrospectively; when referring to a distant day in the future, i.e. "…one day", use *jour*)

> I'll make it one day – *J'y arriverai un jour.* (always *jour* here)

> That day was full of surprises – *Cette journée était remplie de surprises.* (always *journée*)

> It was a clear and sunny day – *C'était une journée ensoleillée et claire.* (weather vocabulary will be presented just after this section about time)

> >>> Note: one of these days, soon – *un de ces jours.*

- Monday – *lundi*

- Tuesday – *mardi*

- Wednesday – *mercredi*

- Thursday – *jeudi*

- Friday – *vendredi*

- Saturday – *samedi*

- Sunday – *dimanche*

- on Sunday, Monday... – *le dimanche, le lundi...*

- a week – *une semaine*

>> He kept on working one week after the other – *Il continua de travailler, une semaine après l'autre.*

>>> to keep on... - *continuer de*

- a weekend – *un week-end*

- a fortnight / two weeks – *quinze jours / deux semaines*

- a month – *un mois*

>> A month had passed by, yet I received no news... – *Un mois s'était écoulé, mais je n'avais pas reçu de nouvelles...*

>>> to pass by – *s'écouler* ("Many years were to pass by before..." – *Beaucoup d'années devaient s'écouler avant que...*)

>>> to fly by – *passer vite* ("Doesn't time always fly by?" – *Est-ce que le temps ne passe pas toujours vite ?*)

- a year – *un an, une année* (similar to the words for "day", uses differ)

>> Happy New Year! – *Bonne année !* (always translated so)

>> I'm 33 years old – *J'ai trente-trois ans* (always translated so)

>> A year has just passed by, but have things really changed? – *Une année / Un an vient de s'écouler, mais est-ce que les choses ont vraiment changé ?* (both are perfectly acceptable)

Last year has been high in emotions – *L'année dernière a été riche en émotions.* (always *année*)

>>> to be high in (emotions; or for food, carbs, proteins...) – *être riche en...* ("be wealthy in", literally).

- six months – *six mois*

- a decade – *une décennie*

> It was undoubtedly a prosperous decade for our company – *C'était sans aucun doute une décennie prospère pour notre entreprise.*

- a century – *un siècle*

> The 21st century is rife with technological advances – *Le XXIème siècle est rempli d'avancées technologiques.*

- a season (of the year) – *une saison*

> There are four seasons in a year – *Il y a quatre saisons dans une année.*

- the spring – *le printemps*

- the summer – *l'été (m)*

> The summer has arrived! – *L'été est arrivé !*

- the autumn – *l'automne (m)*

- the winter – *l'hiver (m)*

- in spring – *au printemps*

- in summer – *en été, à l'été* (both are acceptable, but the first one is slightly more common)

- in autumn, fall – *en automne, à l'automne* (see above: the same applies)

- in winter – *en hiver*

- January – *janvier* (months of the year are never capitalised in French)

- February – *février*

- March – *mars*

- April – *avril*

- May – *mai*
- June – *juin*
- July – *juillet*
- August – *août*
- September – *septembre*
- October – *octobre*
- November – *novembre*
- December – *décembre*
- a holiday – *des vacances* (always plural)
- a public holiday – *un jour férié*
- Easter (Apr 21) – *Pâques*
- Easter Monday (Apr 22) – *le lundi de Pâques*
- Labor Day – *le 1er mai*
- Victory Day – *le 8 mai*
- Ascension Day (May 30) – *l'Ascension*
- Whit day / Pentecost (June 10) – *la Pentecôte, le lundi de Pentecôte*
- Bastille Day – *le 14 juillet*
- Assumption Day – *le 15 août, l'Assomption*
- All Saints' Day (Nov 1st) – *la Toussaint*
- Armistice Day (Nov 11) – *l'Armistice*
- Christmas – *Noël*
- New Year's Day – *le nouvel an*
- to fall on – *tomber (sur)*

    This year, Labor Day falls on a Monday – *Cette année, le 1er mai tombe (sur) un lundi.*

- today – *aujourd'hui*

    Today is always more important than tomorrow – *Aujourd'hui est toujours plus important que demain.*

- yesterday – *hier*

    I unfortunately failed my exam yesterday, but I'll try again later – *J'ai malheureusement raté mon examen hier, mais je réessaierai plus tard.*

- the day before yesterday – *avant-hier*

- tomorrow – *demain*

    Prepare all your suitcases for tomorrow's flight! – *Prépare toutes tes valises pour le vol de demain !*

- the day after tomorrow – *après-demain*

- ages ago – *il y a très longtemps*

    Ages ago, there weren't any cars nor streets around; can you imagine that? – *Il y a très longtemps, il n'y avait pas de voitures ni de rues ; tu peux imaginer ça ?*

- once upon a time – *il était une fois*

    Once upon a time, a blonde princess lived in a big castle – *Il était une fois une princesse blonde qui vivait dans un grand château.*

    >>> In French, "Once upon a time" is not separated from the sentence by a comma, but instead works as a verbal group, hence the French construction: "There was once a blonde princess who lived…"

- once in a blue moon – *tous les trente-six du mois* ("Every 36th day of the month", literally)

    Don't be too hopeful: he only pays rent once in a blue moon! – *Ne sois pas trop optimiste : il paie le loyer seulement tous les trente-six du mois !*

- once – *une fois* (means one time – only one); *dès que* (means "Once something happened …")

> I once left my job without notice because I couldn't stand it anymore – *Une fois, j'ai quitté mon travail sans préavis puisque je ne pouvais plus le supporter.*

> Once he'll have left the town, there won't be anything you can do – *Dès qu'il aura quitté la ville, il n'y aura rien que tu puisses [subj. présent of pouvoir] faire.*

- twice – *deux fois*

Once bitten, twice shy (idiom) – *Chat échaudé craint l'eau froide.*

Click on it twice – *Clique dessus deux fois.*

I won't tell/say it twice… – *Je ne le dirai pas deux fois…*

- before – *avant, auparavant* (slightly more formal and archaic; *auparavant* will be preferred when 'before' isn't followed by anything:)

> I used to work full-time before I moved to this city – *Avant d'emménager / de venir dans cette ville, je travaillais à plein temps.*

> We had never met before – *Nous ne nous étions jamais rencontrés avant / auparavant.*

> \>>> to move somewhere – *emménager dans une maison, un appartement… / venir dans une maison…*

> \>>> to meet someone – *se rencontrer.*

- in my time… – *de mon temps*

> Children weren't so undisciplined in my time! – *Les enfants n'étaient pas indisciplinés de mon temps !*

- after (something) – *après …*

I'll go play some pool after dinner – *J'irai jouer au billard après manger.*

- afterwards – *plus tard*

- later – *plus tard*

I'll come back later – *Je reviendrai plus tard.*

Weather:

All four adjectives below are used in impersonal sentences in French: it's warm – *il fait chaud*

- warm – *chaud*

- hot – *chaud*

- cold – *froid*

>It's pretty cold outside for March – *Il fait plutôt froid dehors pour le mois de mars.*

- freezing – *extrêmement froid ; l'air est / était / sera gelé*

>It was freezing as we stepped onto the platform – *Alors que nous étions en train de monter sur la plateforme, il faisait extrêmement froid / l'air était gelé.*

- sunny – *ensoleillé(e) ; avoir du soleil, faire beau* (in impersonal sentences)

>It was pretty sunny outside, so we decide to eat in the garden – *C'était plutôt ensoleillé dehors / Il y avait pas mal de soleil dehors / Il faisait beau dehors, donc nous avons décidé de manger dans le jardin.*

- the Sun – *le soleil*

- rainy – *pluvieux, -se*

>It was quite a rainy day – *C'était une journée plutôt pluvieuse.*

- rain – *la pluie*

>I'm not really a fan of rain – *Je ne suis pas vraiment fan de la pluie.*

>>> Notice how the noun *fan* is not introduced by an article in French, but instead works like an adjective.

- stormy – *orageux*

- a storm – *un orage, une tempête*

- cloudy – *nuageux*

- a cloud – *un nuage*

- snowy – *enneigée*

- snow – *la neige*

- the sky – *le ciel*

- a drizzle – *du crachin, de la bruine*

> As much as I wanted to go outside, I wasn't willing to face the drizzle – *Autant je voulais aller dehors, autant je ne souhaitais pas affronter le crachin / la bruine.*

- to drizzle – *bruiner*

> Look, it's drizzling outside – *Regarde, il bruine dehors.*

- pouring rain – *une pluie diluvienne*

> I had to wait twenty minutes for my bus in the pouring rain – *J'ai dû attendre mon bus vingt minutes sous une pluie diluvienne.*

- a mist - *un brouillard, une brume*

> What I like the most about living in the mountains is that everything's wrapped in mist in the morning – *Ce que j'aime le plus par rapport au fait de vivre à la montagne, c'est que tout est enveloppé dans du brouillard / dans de la brume le matin.*

Place:

Note: Vocabulary relating to household items and house parts will follow later in Chapter 5.

- a continent – *un continent*

    There are too many continents to explore! – *Il y a trop de continents à explorer !*

- a country – *un pays*
- a region – *une région*

    So, which French region will we pick for our next holidays? – *Alors, quelle région française / région de France allons-nous choisir pour nos prochaines vacances ?*

    >>> to pick (choose between options) – *choisir* (most common), *sélectionner.*

- a province – *une province*
- a house – *une maison*

    She lived in a blue house with green shutters – *Elle vivait dans une maison bleue avec des volets verts.*

- a home – *un foyer*

    I'm glad the puppy found a welcoming home – *Je suis content que le chiot ait trouvé un foyer accueillant.*

- an apartment, a flat – *un appartement* (*appartement* may refer to an individual flat or the whole building; if you wish to be more precise, use *le bâtiment,* 'the building')

    My apartment is on the fourth floor – *Mon appartement est au quatrième / 4ème étage.*

    Can you see those apartment buildings over there? – *Peux-tu voir ces appartements là-bas ?*

- a condo – *un appartement*
- an address – *une adresse*
- a street – *une rue*

So, what's your address? – I live on Marble Street. – *Alors, quelle est ton / votre adresse ? – J'habite sur Marble Street.*

- a neighborhood, a district – *un quartier*

    There are so many delicious bakeries in the neighborhood – *Il y a tellement de boulangeries délicieuses dans le quartier.*

    >>> a bakery – *une boulangerie.*

    >>> there is, there are – *il y a* (both for singular and plural).

- a town – *une ville*
- in town – *en ville*

    I'm going to go to town to do some shopping – *Je vais aller en ville pour faire un peu de shopping.*

- a city – *une ville*
- a metropolis – *une métropole*

    A new metropolis will be built near my town – *Une nouvelle métropole va être construite près de ma ville.*

    >>> to build – *construire* (built, past participate: *construit(e), -s*).

- a capital – *une capitale*
- here – *ici*

    We should meet him here – *Nous devrions le rencontrer ici.*

- over here – *par ici* (as an interjection only), *ici*

    Over here! – *Par ici ! / Ici !*

    Look, your keys are over here – *Regarde, tes clés sont ici.*

- there – *là, là-bas* (*là-bas*, as a rule, tends to be farther away from the speaker than *là*; with *là*, you can generally see the place you're pointing towards, although it is not close to you)

    What's there? – *Qu'est-ce qu'il y a là-bas?*

> The cat was standing just there – *Le chat se tenait debout juste là.*
>
> \>>> to stand – *se tenir debout, être debout*

- over there – *là-bas*

> Look who's sitting over there! – *Regarde qui est assis là-bas !*

- close to… – *près de…* (*près* is invariable)

> My school is close/near to my house – *Mon école est près de ma maison.*

- far from… – *loin de…* (*loin* is invariable)

> The next gas station is very far from here – *La prochaine station essence est très loin d'ici.*
>
> Don't worry, we won't have to walk very far – *Ne t'inquiète pas, nous n'aurons pas à marcher très loin.*
>
> \>>> to worry – *s'inquiète, se préoccuper de…*
>
> \>>> gas station – *station essence* (there is no preposition between the two).

- closer – *plus près*

> Come closer, I don't bite – *Viens plus près, je ne mords pas.*

- further – *plus loin*

- further north, east, south, west – *plus au nord, à l'est, au sud, à l'ouest*

> We got lost here last week: the park was actually further north – *Nous nous sommes perdus ici la semaine dernière : le parc était en fait plus au nord.*

- nearby – *près d'ici*

Maybe there's an open restaurant nearby, who knows? – *Peut-être qu'il y a un restaurant d'ouvert près d'ici, qui sait ? / Il y a peut-être un restaurant...*

- a couple of meters away – *quelques mètres plus loin*

And guess who I saw a couple of meters away? Your brother! – *Et devine qui j'ai vu quelques mètres plus loin ? Ton frère !*

Prepositions – where is this?

- behind... – *derrière*

The bank is just behind this building – *La banque est juste derrière ce bâtiment.*

- in front of – *devant*
- next to – *à côté de*

You'll be sitting next to my cousin -*Tu t'assiéras à côté de mon cousin/ma cousine.*

- above – *au-dessus de* (+ noun), *au-dessus*
- below – *en-dessous de* (+ noun), *en-dessous*
- under – *en-dessous de*

We found the cat under the porch, it was absolutely terrified – *Nous avons trouvé le chat sous le perron, il était absolument terrifié.*

- on (something) – *sur (quelque chose)*

The keys are on the table – *Les clés sont sur la table.*

- in – *dans*

My earrings should be in the box – *Mes boucles d'oreilles devraient être dans la boîte.*

- inside – *dedans*

Come inside, it's getting late – *Viens dedans, il se fait tard.*

>>> it's getting late – *il se fait tard.*

Moving around and being somewhere:

- at, to – *à;* whether you are somewhere or going somewhere:

I'm at the train station *(la gare) – Je suis à la gare.*

I'm going to the train station – *Je vais à la gare.*

- at church, school – *à l'église, à l'école*; note how French always adds an article between *à* and the noun whereas English doesn't:

- at the park, supermarket, beach – *au parc, au supermarché, à la plage*

- at the local fair – *à la fête locale*

- at home – *à la maison*

> I think I'm gonna stay at home all weekend – *Je crois que je vais rester à la maison tout le week-end.*

- on the ground – *au sol, sur le sol* (*au* will denote a movement downwards while *sur le* means it is static)

> He's fallen on the ground – *Il est tombé au sol.* (this is the only possibility)

> There's something on the ground, I can't tell what it is – *Il y a quelque chose sur le sol, je ne sais pas ce que c'est.* (this is the only possibility)

- in, inside – *dans*

- in one's car, house, room, apartment – *dans la voiture, la maison, la chambre, l'appartement de quelqu'un*

- around (the corner) – *au coin de la rue*

- around the house (within the house) – *dans la maison*

> The cat likes to walk around the house and pick up dust – *Le chat aime se promener dans la maison et ramasser de la poussière.*

- around a building (circling outside it) – *autour d'un bâtiment*

> Weeds had spread exponentially around the old deserted factory – *Les mauvaises herbes avaient poussées de façon exponentielle autour de la vieille usine déserte.*

- all around the world – *partout dans le monde, aux quatre coins du monde*

> Moving all around the world in your twenties is an enriching experience – *Bouger aux quatre coins du monde pendant la vingtaine est une expérience enrichissante.*

- on the left – *sur la gauche*
- on the right – *sur la droite*

> You'll definitely recognize the building, it'll be the grey one on the right – *Tu reconnaîtras le bâtiment à coup sûr, ce sera celui en gris / le gris sur la droite.*

> >>> the grey one – French has two ways of expressing this: *celui/celle/ceux/celles* + *en* + adj or noun, or *le/la/les* + adj without any following word: "Did you see the blue one (dress)?" – *Tu as vu la bleue ?)*

> >>> definitely (with complete certainty) – *définitivement, à coup sûr, certainement.*

- from the left / right – *de la gauche / de la droite*

- somewhere – *quelque part*

- somewhere else – *autre part*

Let's go somewhere else – *Allons autre part.*

- anywhere (affirmative) – *n'importe où*

He could be anywhere! – *Il pourrait être n'importe où !*

- anywhere (negative) – *nulle part*

You won't go anywhere dressed like that! – *Tu n'iras nulle part habillé(e) comme ça !*

- nowhere – *nulle part*

> My keys are nowhere to be found – *Je ne trouve mes clés nulle part* (French prefers an active construction here: "I can't find my keys anywhere").

- in the middle of nowhere – *au milieu de nulle part*

> We went camping in the middle of nowhere – *Nous sommes allés camper au milieu de nulle part.*

- everywhere, anywhere (in an affirmative sentence) – *partout, tout autour ; n'importe où* (only for anywhere)

> I lost my keys yesterday morning and have no idea where; they could be anywhere, for all I know – *J'ai perdu mes clés hier matin et je ne sais pas du tout où elles sont / je n'ai aucune idée d'où elles sont ; elles pourraient être n'importe où, pour ce que j'en sais.*

> Following the widespread debate about tiny cameras hidden everywhere around us – *Après le vaste débat sur des minuscules caméras qui seraient cachées tout autour de nous...*

> Seeing violence everywhere can mess with your mind – *Voir de la violence partout / tout autour peut vous affecter la tête / l'esprit / peut vous déranger l'esprit.*

Place – verbs of movement:

- to walk – *marcher*

> We could also walk for a bit, don't you think? – *Nous pourrions aussi marcher un peu, tu ne penses pas ?*

- to wander, roam – *errer, flâner* (note: *errer* tends to have a more melancholic and lonely tone than *flâner*, but the latter stresses a certain kind of laziness too)

> I had never been to Berlin before, and so I wandered in the markets for a whole day – *Je n'étais jamais allé à Berlin*

avant, et j'ai donc erré dans des marchés / flâné dans des marchés pendant toute la journée.

- to visit (a place) – *visiter*

- to run – *courir*

> I run every Monday and Friday – *Je cours tous les lundis et vendredis*

- to jog – *faire du jogging, faire un jogging* (*faire un jogging* is used when you mention only one jogging session; if you're talking about a repeated activity, use *faire du jogging*)

> I like jogging so much – *J'aime tellement faire du jogging.*

> She went for a jog this morning – *Elle a fait un jogging ce matin.*

- to sprint – *sprinter*

- to jump – *sauter*

> He jumped from the diving board and landed in the swimming-pool with a splash – *Il sauta du plongeoir et atterrit dans la piscine avec un "plouf".*

- through – *à travers...*

> He ran through the forest for forty-five minutes – *Il a couru à travers la forêt pendant 45 minutes.*

Chapter 4 – Common Adverbs

Adverbs relating to quantity:

- barely – *à peine*

He could barely speak from the shock – *Il pouvait à peine parler à cause du choc.*

- sufficiently – *suffisamment* ;

I've sufficiently filled the bottles – *J'ai suffisamment rempli les bouteilles.*

>>> to have enough / sufficient (problems, pains, trouble, etc) – *avoir assez / suffisamment de…*

I've got enough trouble getting him to sleep – *J'ai assez / suffisamment de mal à le faire dormir.* ("… to make him sleep", literally).

- enough – *assez*

I've had enough! – *J'en ai assez !*

>>> In French, the simple present tense (avoir: *j'ai*) is always used to translate the present perfect in English.

- drastically – *drastiquement*

He drastically altered his lifestyle after his stroke – *Il changea son mode de vie drastiquement après son AVC.*

- totally – *totalement*

The river totally overflowed its banks – *La rivière est totalement montée en crue.*

>>> to overflow (river, sea) – *monter en crue, être en crue.*

- gradually – *progressivement, graduellement*

Success comes gradually – *Le succès arrive progressivement / graduellement.*

- exponentially – *exponentiellement, de façon exponentielle*

It looked like weeds had sprouted exponentially – *On aurait dit que les mauvaises herbes avaient poussé de façon exponentielle.*

Adverbs relating to quality:

- perfectly – *parfaitement*

What can I say, it was perfectly done! – *Que puis-je dire / Qu'est-ce que je peux dire, ça a été parfaitement fait !*

- superbly – *superbement*

- normally – *normalement*

- poorly – *mal*

Your essay was poorly written – *Ta dissertation était mal écrite.*

- to be poorly read – *ne pas avoir beaucoup de culture*

>>> Also see: to be well-read – *avoir beaucoup de culture.*

- rather (He is rather…) – *plutôt*

I rather had fun there – *Je me suis plutôt bien amusé(e) là-bas.*

>>> "I'd rather…" would be "*Je préférerais / J'aimerais mieux…*" in French.

Adverbs and conjunctions related to time:

- first (when I first did this) – *pour la première fois*
- then – *ensuite*
- finally – *finalement, enfin*
- during – *pendant*

    Don't eat during the show! – *Ne mange pas pendant le spectacle !*

- as (simultaneity) – *pendant que, alors que*

    He spoke to me as I came down the stairs – *Il me parla alors que je descendais les escaliers.*

- while – *pendant que*

    She turned off the lights while I was reading – *Elle a éteint les lumières pendant que j'étais en train de lire.*

- generally – *généralement, la plupart du temps*

    He will generally cut through the park before coming back home – *Il coupera généralement à travers le parc pour revenir à la maison / Il coupera… la plupart du temps.*

- often, oftentimes – *souvent*
- sometimes – *parfois*

    I've sometimes seen my neighbor taking walks in his garden – *J'ai parfois vu mon voisin faire un tour dans son jardin.*

- seldom – *rarement, peu de fois*

    She seldom bothers to garden and clean the house – *Elle s'efforce rarement de jardiner et de nettoyer la maison. / Elle fait rarement l'effort de jardiner…*

>>> to bother doing something – *faire l'effort de faire… / s'efforcer de faire*

- never – *jamais*

   He never touched a glass of alcohol – *Il ne touchait jamais à un verre d'alcool.*

- almost never – *presque jamais*

- definitively – *définitivement ; pour toujours*

   He chose to definitively leave the city – *Il a choisi de quitter la ville définitivement / pour toujours*

- forever – *pour toujours ; à jamais*

Love is forever – *L'amour, c'est pour toujours.*

   He was forever changed from the incident – *L'incident le changea à jamais / Il fut à jamais changé par l'incident.*

   >>> Notice how French privileges an active construction, although the passive one may also be used and understood by natives.

- constantly – *constamment ; tout le temps*

She's constantly busy – *Elle est constamment / tout le temps occupée…*

- periodically – *périodiquement*

   I periodically go for long hikes in the countryside – *Je vais périodiquement faire des randonnées* ("go for hikes") *dans la campagne.*

- regularly – *régulièrement*

Brush your teeth regularly – *Brosse tes dents régulièrement.*

- normally – *normalement*

   He should normally come back at eight – *Il devrait normalement revenir à huit heures.*

- daily, everyday – *tous les jours* (plural, "all the days" literally; you'll also observe this for the following words)

She wakes up at six AM daily – *Il se réveille à six heures tous les jours.*

- once a day – *une fois par jour*

Mail arrives once a day here – *Le courrier arrive une fois par jour ici.*

- weekly, every week – *toutes les semaines*

A fair is organized in town every week – *Une foire est organisée en ville toutes les semaines.*

- once a week – *une fois par semaine*

This class will be scheduled once a week, on Thursdays – *Cette classe sera prévue une fois par semaine, le jeudi.*

>>> to schedule something on a planner: *prévoir quelque chose ; planifier quelque chose.*

- monthly, every month – *tous les mois*

I receive new magazines every month – *Je reçois de nouveaux magasines tous les mois.*

- yearly, every year – *tous les ans*

I grow older every year – *Je deviens plus vieux* ("become older") *tous les ans.*

- once a year – *une fois par an*

He gets a raise once a year – *Il a une augmentation une fois par an.*

Chapter 5 – Houses and Lodgings

- a house – *une maison*

    Can you see the blue house over there? It's mine. – *Est-ce que tu peux voir la maison bleue là-bas ? C'est la mienne.*

- a room (in general) – *une pièce*

    I can't believe we got an apartment with such spacious rooms! – *Je ne peux pas croire que nous ayions trouvé un appartement avec des pièces si spacieuses !*

- a story, a floor – *un étage*

    You'll find the master bedroom on the second floor – *Vous trouverez / Tu trouveras la grande chambre au deuxième étage.*

    It's a two-story house – *C'est une maison à deux étages.*

- stairs – *des escaliers*

- a stairway railing – *une rampe d'escalier*

Hold on tight to the stairway railing, I wouldn't want you to fall down – *Accroche-toi bien fort à la rampe d'escalier, je ne voudrais pas que tu tombes.*

- a lobby – *un vestibule*

    You may leave your coat in the lobby – *Vous pouvez laisser votre manteau dans le vestibule. / Tu peux laisser ton manteau dans le vestibule.*

- a porch – *un porche*

- a terrace – *une terrasse*

- a swimming-pool – *une piscine*

    They built a large terrace next to the swimming-pool. The water is so warm in summer! – *Ils ont construit une large terrasse près de la piscine. L'eau est tellement chaude en été !*

- a front / back garden – *un jardin à l'avant / à l'arrière*

    You'll be most pleased with the house: there's a front garden – *Vous serez extrêmement satisfaits de la maison : il y a un jardin à l'avant.*

- a stoop – *un perron*

    He stopped on the stoop and readjusted his tie – *Il s'arrêta sur le perron et réajusta sa cravate.*

- a mailbox – *une boîte aux lettres*

    Just put it in the mailbox, I'll come pick it up later – *Mettez-le simplement dans la boîte aux lettres, je viendrai le chercher plus tard.*

- the front / back door – *la porte d'entrée* (most common by far), *la porte de devant / la porte de derrière*

- a bell – *une sonnette*

But you didn't even ring the bell before coming in! – *Mais tu n'as même pas appuyé sur la sonnette avant d'entrer !*

>>> to come in (a room, a building) – *rentrer.*

>>> to ring the bell – *appuyer sur la sonnette.*

- a latch – *une chaîne, un loquet*
- a window – *une fenêtre*

    May you open the window? I'm suffocating in here – *Pourrais-tu / Pourriez-vous ouvrir la fenêtre ? Je suffoque ici.*

- open – *ouvrir*
- close – *fermer*
- lock – *fermer à clé*

    I've locked the front door, so in case you want to come in, just ring the bell – *J'ai fermé la porte d'entrée à clé, donc si jamais tu veux rentrer, appuie juste sur la sonnette.*

- a room (in general) – *une pièce*

    There are seven rooms in total in this house – *Il y a sept pièces en tout dans cette maison.*

- the living-room – *le salon*

    Our living-room is pretty spacious – *Notre salle à manger est plutôt spacieuse.*

- a couch – *un sofa, un canapé* (much more common)
- chairs – *des chaises* (singular: *une chaise*)
- a table – *une table*
- a coffee table – *une table basse*

    I had left my magazines on the coffee table, next to the remote control – *J'avais laissé mes magazines sur la table basse, à côté de la télécommande.*

- a TV – *une télévision, une TV*

- a remote control – *une télécommande*

- a cupboard – *une armoire*

- drawers – *des tiroirs* (singular: *un tiroir*)

> Look in the third drawer from the left, it should be there – *Regarde dans le troisième tiroir en partant de la gauche, ça devrait être là.*

> \>>> from the left / right / top / bottom (when picking one item out of a succession) – *en partant de la gauche / de la droite / du haut / du bas.*

> I want the fourth dress from the top on that rack – *Je veux la quatrième robe en partant du haut sur cette étagère.*

- a carpet – *un tapis*

- a kitchen – *une cuisine*

- to cook - *cuisiner*

- a fridge – *un réfrigérateur, un frigo* (much more common)

> I've put the milk in the fridge – *J'ai mis le lait dans le frigo.*

- a freezer – *un congélateur, un congélo* (more common)

> There is some ice-cream in the freezer – *Il y a des glaces dans le congélo.*

> \>>> an ice-cream – *une glace* (not to be confused with ice – *de la glace*), (plural) *des glaces.*

- a sink – *un évier*

- a tap, faucet – *un robinet*

> Someone should turn off the tap, I can hear water slop in the sink – *Quelqu'un devrait fermer le robinet, je peux entendre l'eau clapoter dans l'évier.*

- turn on, turn off a tap – *ouvrir, fermer un robinet*

- a microwave oven – *un four à micro-ondes*, commonly abbreviated as *un micro-ondes*

- an oven – *un four*

- the thermostat – *le thermostat*

- a frying pan – *une poêle à frire,* commonly abbreviated as *une poêle*

- a saucer, saucepan – *une casserole*

- boiling water – *de l'eau bouillante*

>>> to boil (water, blood) – *bouillir.*

- a dining-room – *la salle à manger*

- a plate – *une assiette*

- a fork – *une fourchette*

- a knife – *un couteau*

>>> see related verbs: to cut – *couper*; to chop (i.e. vegetables) – *couper des légumes.*

- a spoon – *une cuillère*

>>> a spoonful – *une cuillerée.*

- a glass – *un verre*

There were many plates and glasses in the sink – *Il y avait beaucoup d'assiettes et de verres dans l'évier.*

- a jug, a pitcher – *un pichet, une cruche*

Can you bring us a pitcher for the lemonade? – *Pouvez-vous / Peux-tu nous amener un pichet / une cruche pour la limonade ?*

- cutlery – *des couverts*

- a teaspoon – *une cuillère à café*

- a tablespoon – *une cuillère à soupe*

You should now add two tablespoons of sugar and stir well – *Vous devriez maintenant ajouter deux cuillères à soupe de sucre et bien mélanger.*

>>> to stir – *mélanger, touiller* (the second is much more informal and idiomatic)

- sugar – *du sucre*

- salt – *du sel*

- pepper – *du poivre*

- to salt – *saler*

- to pepper – *poivrer*

- a bathroom (shower/bath) – *une salle de bain*

- the bathroom – *les toilettes, les WC*

- a bath – *un bain*

- a shower – *une douche*

- a towel – *une serviette*

- to dry oneself (with a towel) – *se sécher (avec une serviette)*

- a room (to sleep in) – *une chambre, une chambre à coucher* (the abbreviated version is much more common)

I'll now show you your room – *Je vais maintenant vous montrer votre chambre.*

- a bed – *un lit*

- a bedside table – *une table de nuit*

- a lamp – *une lampe*

- a lightbulb – *une ampoule*

I have to replace this lightbulb – *Je dois remplacer cette ampoule.*

Electrical appliances:

- electricity, power – *de l'électricité*

- fuses – *des fusibles*

- the light – *la lumière, les lumières* (the concept of "light" will rather be in the infinitive)

- to turn on, turn off the lights – *allumer, éteindre les lumières*

- a switch – *un interrupteur*

- to switch on, switch off the lights – *allumer, éteindre les lumières (avec un interrupteur*; may be omitted if it is clear)

> Switch off the lights over there please – *Eteins les lumières là-bas, s'il te plaît.*

- a curfew – *un couvre-feu*

- a socket – *une prise*

- a plug – *une prise*

> You'll find plugs under the desk, on your right – *Vous trouverez des prises sous le bureau, à votre droite.*

- a cable – *un câble*

- to plug in a cable – *brancher un câble*

- an adapter – *un adaptateur*

> Don't forget to bring an adapter to be able to charge your things – *N'oublie pas d'amener un adaptateur pour pouvoir charger tes objets.*

- to (re)charge – *(re)charger*

> Looks like the computer needs charging – *On dirait que l'ordinateur a besoin d'être chargé / a besoin de batterie.*

Chapter 6 – Common French Verbs: an Overview

- accept – *accepter*

> So far, he hasn't accepted my excuses – *Jusque là, il n'a pas accepté mes excuses.*

> >>> so far – *jusque là, jusqu'ici, jusqu'à maintenant.* The three of them can be used when speaking about time, as within the example; when you're mentioning distance, i.e. I didn't think we would walk so far, you may use *jusqu'ici, jusque là*, ou *si loin*.

- accuse – *accuser*

> He was accused of embezzling from the company before they found the real culprit – *Il a été accusé d'avoir volé de l'argent à l'entreprise avant que l'on ne retrouve le vrai coupable.*

> >>> In instances where there is an unexplained subject in English that doesn't carry a lot of meaning (e.g. "They found the real culprit"), French will privilege using *on*.

- achieve – *faire, obtenir*

    I'm proud of myself because I managed to achieve so much during the past year – *Je suis fier de moi parce que j'ai réussi à faire tant de choses pendant cette année.*

    He's achieved the best score possible on his SATs – *il a obtenu le meilleur score possible à son brevet des collèges / baccalauréat* (the *brevet des collèges* test is when students are around sixteen years old, or *baccalauréat*, shortened to *bac*, is taken just before university).

- acknowledge – *reconnaître*

    I must acknowledge that his attention to detail is outstanding – *Je dois reconnaître que son souci du détail est remarquable.*

- act (do something) – *agir*

    He always acts for others and likes helping people – *Il agit toujours pour les autres et il aime aider les gens.*

- act (do some acting) – *être acteur, être actrice*

    My aunt's been acting for twenty years – *Cela fait vingt ans que ma tante est actrice.*

- act (behave) – *se comporter*

    They all acted weird because of a superstition – *Ils se comportaient tous étrangement à cause d'une superstition.*

- admire – *admirer*

    What I admire most about this company is their work environment – *Ce que j'admire le plus chez cette société / entreprise, c'est leur environnement de travail.*

- admit – *admettre*

    I'll have to admit, your cooking is phenomenal! – *Je dois admettre que votre cuisine est phénoménale !*

>>> cooking (activity, craft) – *la cuisine*

- adopt (a pet, child; a law) – *adopter*

    They adopted a puppy for their daughter – *Ils ont adopté un chiot pour leur fille.*

    A new law was adopted in Parliament – *Une nouvelle loi a été adoptée au Parlement / Le Parlement a adopté une nouvelle loi.*

- adore – *adorer*

    I adored our last trip to Paris – *J'ai adoré notre dernier voyage à Paris.*

- advise – *conseiller*

    May I only advise you to stay away from those rascals – *Puis-je seulement te conseiller de rester loin de ces chenapans / de ne pas t'approcher de ces chenapans.*

- afford – *se permettre*

    I wish I could afford a more lavish lifestyle, but hopefully that'll be the case in a couple of years – *J'aimerais me permettre un style de vie plus luxueux, mais avec de la chance cela sera le cas dans quelques années.*

    >>> I wish... – *J'aimerais; si seulement* (refer to "wish" directly in this list).

    >>> hopefully – *avec de la chance, avec un peu de chance, en croisant les doigts* ("crossing one's fingers").

- allow – *permettre, autoriser*

    Perhaps if I'm nice with her, she'll allow me to go to that party next Saturday? – *Peut-être que si je suis gentil avec elle, elle me permettra / m'autorisera à aller à cette fête samedi prochain ?*

Smoking is not allowed except in designated areas – *Fumer n'est pas permis / autorisé, sauf dans les zones prévues.*

>>> Pay attention: an "allowance" is *une allocation, une indemnité* in French.

- apologize – *s'excuser, demander pardon*

    I must apologize for the intrusion, but… – *Je vous prie de m'excuser / Je vous demande pardon pour cette intrusion, mais…*

    Once he realized his mistake, he apologised profusely – *Dès qu'il se rendit compte de son erreur, il s'excusa abondamment.*

- appear (suddenly show up) – *apparaître*

    A frightening shadow appeared in between the trees, and was gone the next second – *Une ombre effrayante apparut entre les arbres, et avait disparu la seconde suivante.*

    >>> frightening – *effrayante.*

- appear (of a person or thing: seem, look) – *paraître*

    He appeared particularly tired from his long journey – *Il paraissait particulièrement fatigué à cause de son long voyage.*

    This window appears broken – *Cette fenêtre paraît cassée.*

- appear (it appears/seems that…) – *il apparaît que…*

    It appeared that we had been looking at the wrong person all along – *Il apparut que nous avions regardé la mauvaise personne tout ce temps.*

    >>> all along – *pendant tout ce temps, tout ce temps.*

- approach – *s'approcher*

    The small cat approached with caution – *Le petit chat s'approcha avec prudence.*

- argue (put forth arguments) – *argumenter*

    You never listen, it's simply impossible to argue with you! – *Tu n'écoutes jamais, c'est tout simplement impossible d'argumenter avec toi !*

- argue (get in a fight) – *se disputer*

    The neighbors are still arguing... – *Les voisins sont encore en train de se disputer...*

- arrive – *arriver*

    He suddenly arrived as the clock struck midnight – *Il arriva soudainement alors que la pendule affichait minuit.*

- ask – *demander*

    You could have at least asked me before! – *Tu aurais au moins pu me demander avant !*

    >>> at least / at most – *au moins / tout au plus* ("He has at most three pairs of shoes" – *il a tout au plus trois paires de chaussures*).

    May I ask you something? – *Puis-je vous / te demander quelque chose ?*

- assist – *assister* (has largely fallen out of use), *aider*

    She assisted me for planning our trip to Spain – *Elle m'a aidé pour planifier notre voyage en Espagne.*

- assure – *assurer*

    I can assure you that I had no idea he would arrive that late! – *Je peux t'assurer / vous assurer que je n'avais aucune idée du fait qu'il arriverait si tard / que je ne savais pas du tout qu'il arriverait si tard.*

- avoid – *éviter*

He would do anything to avoid helping around the house – *Il ferait n'importe quoi afin d'éviter de donner un coup de main dans la maison.*

- be – *être*

    I'm currently at the train station – *Je suis à la gare en ce moment.*

    I am so tired – *Je suis si fatigué.*

    >>> However: "I'm twenty-two years old" – *J'ai vingt-deux ans.* (French will always use *avoir* when telling your age, so be careful).

- be, feel bored – *s'ennuyer*

    I feel bored whenever I'm alone – *Dès que je suis seul(e), je m'ennuie.*

    He's often tired when he comes back from work – *Il est souvent fatigué quand il rentre du travail.*

- become – *devenir*

    I'd like to become a renowned scientist when I grow up – *J'aimerais devenir un scientifique connu / de renom quand je serai plus grand.*

    >>> renowned: *connu, de renom*

    I can't believe he's become so different – *Je ne peux pas croire qu'il soit devenu si différent.*

    >>> *soit*, here, is the subjunctive present of *être* (*que je sois, que tu sois, qu'il/elle soit, que nous soyons, que vous soyez, qu'ils soient*).

- believe – *croire*

    Do you believe in ghosts? – *Est-ce que tu crois aux fantômes ?*

- beg – *supplier*

Must I beg you to open the door, or go and sleep elsewhere? – *Dois-je te supplier d'ouvrir la porte, ou aller dormir autre part ?*

- begin – *commencer* (most common), *débuter* (formal, somewhat old-fashioned)

> The show will begin soon – *Le spectacle commencera / débutera bientôt.*

- bet – *parier*

> I bet he'll forget his coat once again – *Je parie qu'il oubliera son manteau encore une fois.*

> >>> once again – *encore une fois, une fois de plus, une nouvelle fois* (all three expressions are similar in register and use).

- botch (slang) – *rater (un travail, projet, une coiffure* – when the whole project is undermined*); bâcler (des devoirs, un projet* – when it isn't completely finished, or one hasn't put in a lot of effort*)*

> The hairdresser completely botched my perm – *Le coiffeur / La coiffeuse a totalement raté ma permanente.*

> I think I've botched my exam – *Je crois que j'ai raté mon examen.*

> It's obvious he didn't care about his homework and botched it – *C'est évident qu'il ne se souciait pas de ses devoirs et les a bâclés.*

> >>> homework – *des devoirs*, always in the plural in French.

- bother (someone, something) – *déranger*

> Does this bother you? – *Est-ce que ça vous dérange ?*

- bother doing… – *prendre la peine de faire…*

> He didn't even bother to call me – *Il n'a même pas pris la peine de m'appeler.*

- break (an item) – *briser, casser*

    He broke my heart – *Il m'a brisé le coeur.*

    The glass unexpectedly broke – *Le verre s'est brisé sans prévenir.*

- break (leg, arm) – *se casser*

    She broke her wrist – *Elle s'est cassé le poignet.*

    Stop running around like that or you'll break some bones! – *Arrête de courir dans tous les sens comme ça ou tu te casseras des os !*

- break down (explain) – *séparer en, être constitué de*

    Your essay should be broken down into four different parts – *Votre dissertation devrait être séparée en / constituée de quatre parties différentes.*

- break down (have a breakdown) – *éclater en sanglots* (burst into tears)

    He broke down unexpectedly in the middle of a meeting – *Soudainement, il éclata en sanglots en plein milieu d'une réunion.*

- break down (stop working) – *cesser de fonctionner, tomber en panne* (the second option is much more used when it comes to cars, engines and machinery)

    My car broke down on the way home – *Ma voiture est tombée en panne tandis que je revenais à la maison / chez moi.*

- break up (end a relationship) – *se séparer*

    My parents broke up when I was ten – *Mes parents se sont séparés quand j'avais dix ans.*

- bring (someone somewhere) – *emmener (quelqu'un quelque part)*

What about I bring you to the supermarket instead? – *Et pourquoi je ne t'emmènerai pas au supermarché plutôt ?*

He brought her home – *Il l'a ramenée à la maison.*

- bring (something) – *amener (quelque chose)*

I brought you a little something to help you cope – *Je t'ai amené un petit quelque chose pour t'aider à surmonter tout ça.*

- build – *construire*

She built two houses in only six months: that's quite impressive! – *Elle a construit deux maisons en seulement six mois : c'est assez impressionnant !*

- buy – *acheter*

I have to buy some supplies at the local supermarket – *Je dois acheter quelques marchandises au supermarché du coin.*

- call (on the phone, out loud) – *appeler*

Uncle Patrick called this morning – *L'oncle Patrick a appelé ce matin.*

I haven't stopped calling his name but he won't turn around – *Je n'ai pas arrêté de l'appeler par son nom mais il ne voulait pas se retourner.*

- catch (an item, a disease) – *attraper*

He catches the flu every winter – *Il attrape un rhume tous les hivers.*

>>> the flu – *un rhume* (to catch the flu); *le rhume* (the flu is an infectious disease…)

- catch up – *se tenir au courant ; se revoir*

Let's catch up another time! – *Revoyons-nous une autre fois !*

I like to catch up with current news – *J'aime me tenir au courant des nouvelles actuelles.*

- cause – *causer*

    Eating a lot of sugar causes energy spikes – *Manger beaucoup de sucre cause des pics d'énergie.*

- cease – *cesser*

    This folly must cease! – *Cette folie doit cesser !*

- choose – *choisir*

    The time has now come to choose between this one or that one – *Le temps est maintenant venu de choisir entre celui-ci et celui-là.*

- cling to (physically; to the past; to an idea) – *s'accrocher à*

    The cat clung onto the wall before falling down – *Le chat s'est accroché au mur avant de tomber.*

    He clings to that idea as though it were the only possible solution – *Il s'accroche à cette idée comme si c'était la seule solution possible.*

- clink – *cliqueter*

    As he moved around, his keys clinked in his bag – *Alors qu'il bougeait, ses clés cliquetaient dans son sac.*

- close – *fermer*

    He violently closed the door and left – *Il ferma violemment la porte et partit.*

- close up on – *se rapprocher de*

    She was closing up on her goal – *Elle se rapprochait de son objectif.*

- collaborate – *collaborer*

    We collaborated with another team to finish the project – *Nous avons collaboré avec une autre équipe pour terminer le projet.*

- come (arrive, without noting the means of transportation) – *venir*

    I won't be able to come until 6:00 PM because of an important meeting – *Je ne pourrai pas venir avant dix-huit heures à cause d'une réunion importante.*

- come (by bus, train...) – *venir, arriver*

    He has just come by bus after a long journey through the countryside – *Il vient juste d'arriver en bus après un long voyage à travers la campagne.*

    I'll come by train – *Je viendrai en train.*

    >>> I have just... – *Je viens juste de...* (which is also why it was *arriver* that was used in the first sentence, otherwise it would be extremely redundant)

- come in, come inside – *rentrer, entrer*

    Please, do come in! – *Je vous en prie, rentrez ! / entrez !*

    He came inside the building, drenched with rain – *Il est entré / rentré dans le bâtiment, trempé par la pluie.*

- Come on! – *Viens ! / Vas-y !*

- come out (be revealed) – *être révélé*

    The truth will eventually come out – *Tôt ou tard, la vérité sera révélée.*

- come out (words) – *sortir*

    I can't believe a word that comes out of his mouth – *Je ne peux pas croire un mot qui sort de sa bouche.*

- come outside – *venir dehors*

    You should all come outside, the view is breathtaking! – *Vous devriez tous venir dehors, la vue est à couper le souffle !*

    >>> breathtaking – *à couper le souffle* (from to take one's breath away – *couper le souffle à quelqu'un*).

- come to a halt – *s'arrêter, cesser*

    Although recent sales had surged, the game's popularity came to a halt – *Même si les ventes récentes avaient fortement augmentées, la popularité du jeu s'arrêta.*

- come up (guess, discover) – *trouver*

    He managed to come up with a handy solution in less than ten minutes – *Il a réussi à trouver une solution élégante en moins de dix minutes.*

- compare – *comparer*

    I always make it a point to compare different products before making my mind – *Je prends toujours le soin de comparer entre différents produits avant de prendre une décision.*

    >>> to make it a point to… – *prendre le soin de, faire l'effort de.*

    >>> to make up one's mind – *prendre une décision, faire un choix.*

- complain – *se plaindre*

    Will you stop complaining for once? – *Vas-tu arrêter de te plaindre pour une fois ?*

    We received complaints after the party – *Nous avons reçu des plaintes après la fête.*

- control – *contrôler*

    Although I know you like controlling what's going on, that won't work here – *Même si je sais que tu aimes contrôler ce qui arrive, ça ne marchera pas ici.*

    >>> … what's going on – *ce qui se passe*

    >>> What's going on? – *Que se passe-t-il ? / Qu'est-ce qu'il se passe ?*

- consider (weigh options) – *considérer l'idée que, penser à*

Did you consider the fact that it may not work? – *As-tu considéré l'idée que ça pourrait ne pas marcher ? / As-tu pensé au fait que ça pourrait ne pas marcher ?*

- continue – *continuer*

    The show will continue during the afternoon – *Le spectacle continuera pendant l'après-midi.*

- convince – *convaincre*

    I had to convince him that moving abroad was the best solution – *J'ai dû le convaincre que partir à l'étranger était la meilleure solution.*

- cook – *cuisiner*

    She particularly likes cooking for guests and friends – *Elle aime particulièrement cuisiner pour des invités et des amis.*

    Cooking has already been a passion of mine – *La cuisine a toujours été une de mes passions.* (note how the French translates that as "one of my passions", literally).

- copy – *copier*

    His essay was mostly copy and paste – *Sa dissertation est en majeure partie du copier-coller.*

- cost – *coûter*

    How much does this lamp cost? – *Combien coûte cette lampe ?*

    That'll cost you 20€ in total – *Cela vous coûtera 20€ au total.*

- create – *créer*

    I like creating short movies in my spare time – *J'aime créer des courts-métrages dans mon temps libre.*

- criticize – *critiquer*

    I like to criticize everything – *J'aime tout critiquer.*

- cry – *pleurer*

    She cried during the entire funeral – *Elle a pleuré pendant tout l'enterrement.*

- crumble – *s'effondrer*

    The plan crumbled, and we didn't see it coming – *Le plan s'est effondré, et nous ne l'avons pas vu venir.*

    >>> to see something coming – *voir quelque chose venir.*

- decide – *décider*

    You have to decide whether or not to pursue your ambitions – *Il faut que tu décides si oui ou non tu veux poursuivre tes ambitions.*

- deny – *nier*

    One day he'll stop denying he knew them – *Un jour, il arrêtera de nier qu'il les connaissait.*

- describe – *décrire*

    If I were to describe my dream life, it would be… - *Si je devais décrire la vie de mes rêves, ce serait…*

- disagree – *ne pas être d'accord*

    I disagree with your conclusion because… – *Je ne suis pas d'accord avec votre conclusion parce que…*

- disappear – *disparaître*

    It seemed as though everybody had disappeared – *On aurait dit que tout le monde avait disparu.*

- discuss – *discuter de*

    We discussed a couple of options before moving forward – *Nous avons discuté de quelques options avant d'avancer.*

- dissipate – se *dissiper*

His anger dissipated gradually – *Sa colère s'est dissipée progressivement.*

- do the dishes, the laundry, the cooking – *faire la vaisselle, la lessive, la cuisine*

> Why should I always be the one that does all the cooking? – *Pourquoi est-ce que ça devrait toujours être moi qui fait toute la cuisine ?*

- do good – *faire le bien*

> She's always liked doing good for her fellow neighbors – *Elle a toujours aimé faire le bien pour ses voisins.*

- do nothing – *ne rien faire*

> So what, we'll just sit here and do nothing? – *Alors quoi, on va juste rester assis ici et ne rien faire ?*

- do (in the general sense) – *faire des choses*

> He likes doing things – *Il aime faire des choses.*

- doubt – *douter*

> She doubts their sincerity – *Elle doute de leur sincérité.*
>
> I doubt he'll make it on time – *Je doute qu'il arrive à temps.*

- dream – *rêver*

> When he was a child, he would always be dreaming about building a cabin in the forest – *Quand il était enfant, il rêvait toujours de construire une cabine dans la forêt.*

- drive – *conduire*

> Can you let me drive for once? – *Peux-tu me laisser conduire, pour une fois ?*
>
> >>> for once – *pour une fois.*

- eat – *manger*

> You could also eat at this restaurant, I've heard good things about it – *Vous pourriez également manger dans ce restaurant, j'ai entendu de bonnes choses à son propos.*

> So, what are we eating tonight? – *Alors, qu'est-ce qu'on mange ce soir ?*

- eliminate – *éliminer*

> The nation's favorite contestant was eliminated from a popular TV show – *Le participant le plus aimé du pays a été éliminé d'une télé-réalité populaire.*

- enjoy – *aimer, apprécier*

> I really enjoyed yesterday's evening at the zoo – *J'ai vraiment apprécié la soirée d'hier au zoo.*

- erase – *effacer*

> He'd rather erase this from his memory – *Il préférerait effacer ça de sa mémoire.*

> I've accidentally erased your number from my phone; what was it again? – *J'ai effacé ton numéro de mon téléphone accidentellement ; c'était quoi, déjà ?*

- exist – *exister; exister* also often serves as a translation for "there is", "there are" (*il existe*)

> Pretending that something doesn't exist won't make it go away – *Prétendre que quelque chose n'existe pas ne va pas le faire disparaître.*

> There are many more diseases in poor and underdeveloped countries – *Il existe beaucoup plus de maladies dans des pays pauvres et sous-développés.*

- expect – *s'attendre à*

> I don't see why I should expect any sympathy from her – *Je ne vois pas pourquoi je devrais m'attendre à la moindre sympathie de sa part.*

- fall down – *tomber*

    He fell down the stairs and broke his left hip – *Il est tombé dans les escaliers et s'est cassé la hanche gauche.*

- fall out (get into an argument, not talk anymore) – *s'être brouillé* (the verb is pronominal in French to put forth the fact that the situation is mutual, happens to both parties)

    Brian and his father fell out – *Brian et son père se sont brouillés.*

- fear – *avoir peur de* (may also translated as "be afraid of")

    I fear we'll have to make hard decisions – *J'ai peur que nous devions prendre des décisions difficiles.*

- feel (emotions) – *ressentir*

    How does that make you feel? – I don't know. – *Qu'est-ce que tu ressens par rapport à ça ? – Je ne sais pas.*

- feel (+ adjective, i.e. weird, happy) – *se sentir*

    He felt so happy when he saw them – *Il s'est senti si heureux quand il les a vus.*

- fight (someone else, a disease) – *se battre contre*

    Stop fighting! – *Arrêtez de vous battre !*

- find – *trouver*

    I finally found the solution to your problem – *J'ai enfin trouvé la solution à ton problème.*

- follow – *suivre*

    I think I'll follow my own advice – *Je pense que je suivrai mes propres conseils.*

    >>> a piece of advice, advice – *un conseil, des conseils.*

    The dog was following the baker – *Le chien suivait le boulanger.*

- forget – *oublier* (it doesn't require any preposition after it in French)

> Have you forgotten about our appointment? – *As-tu oublié notre rendez-vous ?*

- gain – *gagner* (in general); *prendre* (*du poids*, weight)

> I've gained so much weight during the holidays – *J'ai pris tant de poids pendant les vacances.*

> What will I gain from that? – *Qu'est-ce que je vais gagner grâce à ça ?*

- garner – *recevoir* (in active sentences) ; *valoir* (in passive sentences)

> His many achievements garnered a lot of praise – *Ses nombreux accomplissements lui ont valu beaucoup de louanges. / Il a reçu beaucoup de louanges suite à ses nombreux accomplissements.*

> \>>> praise – *des louanges, des éloges.*

- give – *donner*

> I'll give him some new clothes once I get back. – *Je lui donnerai de nouveaux vêtements dès que je reviens.*

> Give me one! – *Donne-m'en une !*

- give in, give up – *abandonner*

> I give up, it's too difficult for me – *J'abandonne, c'est trop dur pour moi.*

- go – *aller*

> He pestered us to go to Italy for the summer – *Il ne nous a pas lâchés pour aller en Italie pour l'été.*

- go away – *disparaître, cesser ;* (leave) *partir*

It's just a matter of minutes before the pain goes away – *Il ne va falloir que quelques minutes avant que la douleur ne disparaisse.*

Go away now! – *Pars maintenant !*

- go over – *regarder, consulter*

Let us go over our budget for the year – *Regardons notre budget pour l'année.*

I had to go over several hundred books before finding the one I wanted – *J'ai dû regarder / consulter des centaines de livres avant de trouver celui que je veux.*

>>> several hundred… – *plusieurs centaines de*

- happen – *se passer, se produire*

What happened? – *Qu'est-ce qui s'est passé ? / Que s'est-il produit ?* (this second option is more for use in formal reports, e.g. questions from police/doctors.)

What happens now? – *Qu'est-ce qui se passe maintenant ?*

- have – *avoir*

They have many supplies for travelers, so we should find everything we need – *Ils ont beaucoup de marchandises pour les voyageurs, donc nous devrions trouver tout ce dont nous avons besoin.*

- have something in mind – *avoir quelque chose à l'esprit / en tête*

He was walking around confidently, as though he had something in mind – *Il marchait avec confiance, comme s'il avait quelque chose à l'esprit / en tête.*

- have time on one's hands – *avoir du temps de libre, avoir du temps à consacrer à…*

I'll have enough time on my hands to take care of the cat – *J'aurai assez de temps libre pour m'occuper du chat.*

- have a case of ... – *être en présence d'un cas de...*

> We obviously have a case of intense paranoia here – *Nous sommes de toute évidence en présence d'un cas de paranoïa intense ici.*

- hear – *entendre*

> Have you heard the news? – *As-tu entendu la nouvelle ?*

> Speak louder, I can't hear you – *Parle plus fort, je ne t'entends pas.*

- hide – *cacher*

> He would hide his tantrums from us – *Il avait l'habitude de nous cacher ses crises de colère.*

- hope – *espérer*

> I hope you packed enough food – *J'espère que tu as pris assez de nourriture.*

> >>> I should hope so – *Je l'espère.*

- hurry – *se dépêcher*

> Hurry up, or you're gonna miss the train! – *Dépêche-toi, ou tu vas rater le train !*

- ignore – *ignorer*

> He's been ignoring the dishes for too long – *Cela fait trop longtemps qu'il ignore la vaisselle.*

- impress – *impressionner*

> He impresses me with his cooking skills – *Il m'impressionne avec ses talents de cuisinier.*

- increase – *augmenter*

> Our sales greatly increased during the last quarter – *Nos ventes ont beaucoup augmenté durant les trois derniers mois.*

>>> during the next / last quarter – *durant les trois prochains mois / durant les trois derniers mois.*

- inform – *informer*

    I have just been informed of violent riots in town – *On vient juste de m'informer au sujet de manifestations violentes en ville.*

- insist – *insister*

    But you'll stay here for the night, I insist – *Mais tu resteras ici pour la nuit, j'insiste.*

- justify – *justifier*

    I will probably have to justify my decision, what do you think? – *Je devrai probablement justifier ma décision, qu'est-ce que tu en penses ?*

- keep – *garder, conserver*

    I've finally chosen to keep that scarf – *J'ai finalement choisi de garder cette écharpe.*

- keep a secret – *garder un secret*

    Can you keep a secret? – *Peux-tu garder un secret ?*

- keep a promise – *tenir une promesse*

    I'll keep that promise – *Je tiendrai cette promesse.*

- keep on… – *continuer de…*

    She'll keep on working until she collapses – *Elle continuera de travailler jusqu'à ce qu'elle s'effondre.*

- know – *savoir*

    Of course I know how to do that! – *Bien sûr que je sais comment faire ça !*

- laugh – *rire*

> She burst out laughing during the funeral – *Elle a éclaté de rire pendant l'enterrement.*

- learn – *apprendre*

> You first learn to count and read in school – *On apprend d'abord à compter et à lire à l'école.*

- leave – *partir*

> I've got to leave now – *Je dois partir maintenant.*

- lie – *mentir*

> Even though he always lies, I suppose we can trust him – *Même s'il ment tout le temps, je suppose que nous pouvons lui faire confiance.*

- lie down – *s'allonger*

> I'm a bit tired, I've got to lie down – *Je suis un peu fatigué(e), il faut que je m'allonge.*

> >>> I've got to… – *il faut que* (most common); *je dois* (when you are given an order).

- like – *aimer*

> She likes travelling and taking pictures – *Elle aime voyager et prendre des photos.*

- look – *regarder*

> He briefly looked at what was going on outside, then went out – *Il regarda brièvement ce qui se passait au-dehors, puis sortit.*

> Look! – *Regarde !*

- lose – *perdre*

> I don't want to lose any more time on this – *Je ne veux pas perdre plus de temps sur ça.*

- love – *aimer*

Don't you love swimming at night? – *Est-ce que tu n'aimes pas nager la nuit ?*

- make – depending on the context:

1. make an item: *créer, faire*

> I made this polka dress for you – *J'ai fait cette robe à pois pour toi.*
>
> Won't you make some coffee for our guests? – *Ne vas-tu pas faire du café pour nos invités ?*

2. make money – *gagner*

> I've never made that much money before – *Je n'ai jamais gagné autant d'argent auparavant.*

- make up (invent) – *inventer*

> My uncle was great: he would always make up incredible stories – *Mon oncle, c'était quelqu'un de génial : il inventait toujours des histoires incroyables.*

- make up (reconcile) – *se réconcilier*

> It looks like the two friends made up during the weekend – *On dirait que les deux amis se sont réconciliés pendant le week-end.*

- manage (run) – *gérer*

> He managed the whole company without blinking an eye – *Il géra toute l'entreprise sans sourciller.*

- may – *pouvoir*

> May I introduce you to my father? – *Puis-je vous présenter à mon père ?*
>
> I may not be able to come – *Il se peut que je ne puisse pas venir.*
>
> This may seem impolite, but... – *Cela peut sembler malpoli, mais...*

- mean (signify) – *vouloir dire*

    What did you mean when you said that? – *Que voulais-tu dire quand tu as dit ça ?*

- meet (for the first time) – *rencontrer*

    So, where did you two meet? – *Alors, où vous êtes-vous rencontrés / où est-ce que vous vous êtes rencontrés ?*

- might – *pouvoir* in the conditional mood (*je pourrais, tu pourrais, il/elle pourrait, nous pourrions, vous pourriez, ils/elles pourraient*)

    She might not be there when you come back – *Il se pourrait qu'elle ne soit pas là quand tu reviendras / vous reviendrez.*

- mince (meat) – *émincer*

    Do you think we need some minced meat for the pie? – *Penses-tu qu'on ait besoin de viande émincée pour la tourte?*

- mince one's words – *mâcher ses mots*

    He's definitely not one to mince his words – *Ce n'est définitivement pas le genre à mâcher ses mots.*

- miss – *manquer* ; particularly pay attention to how the French say it:

    I miss you – *Tu me manques.*

    I miss my old friends – *Mes anciens amis me manquent.*

- mourn – *regretter; faire le deuil de*

    She took two weeks off to mourn the death of her husband – *Il a pris deux semaines de vacances pour faire le deuil du décès de son mari.*

    I still mourn the way it ended – *Je regrette toujours la façon dont ça s'est terminé.*

- move – *bouger*

    Don't move! – *Ne bougez pas !*

- move in – *s'installer*

    He moved in two weeks ago – *Il s'est installé il y a deux semaines.*

- move on (from an event) – *passer à autre chose*

    Stop dwelling on the past and move on – *Arrête de t'apesantir sur le passé / de t'accrocher au passé et passe à autre chose.*

- move on (during a presentation) – *avancer*

    Now that we all agree on that, let's move on – *Maintenant que nous sommes tous d'accord sur ça, avançons.*

- move to (live somewhere else) – *partir pour, s'installer à, partir s'installer à*

    He moved to San Francisco – *Il est parti pour San Francisco / s'est installé à SF / est parti s'installer à SF.*

- move up (the ladder) – *progresser*

    Thanks to his dedication, he moved up the ladder and got a good position – *Grâce à son travail acharné, il a progressé et obtenu un bon poste.*

    >>> dedication – *travail acharné.*

- observe – *observer*

    He was observing butterflies and birds – *Il observait des papillons et des oiseaux.*

- offer – *offrir*

    I offered him a sandwich, but he declined – *Je lui ai offert un sandwich, mais il a refusé.*

- order (food, drinks) – *commander*

    She ordered two drinks – *Elle a commandé deux boissons.*

- perceive – *percevoir*

Human eyes can perceive a great spectrum of colors – *Les yeux humains peuvent percevoir un large éventail de couleurs.*

- pretend – *prétendre*

I won't pretend I didn't know – *Je ne prétendrai pas que je ne savais pas.*

- pull the door – *tirer la porte* (whereas "push the door" is: *pousser la porte*)

Note: *pousser la porte* is also an idiom that means "visit someone", "come somewhere".

Don't hesitate to come visit us while you're in France! – *N'hésitez pas à pousser la porte / nous rendre visite pendant que vous êtes en France !*

Pull the door to enter – *Tirez la porte pour entrer.*

- pull the plug – *déconnecter*

I'll finally get to pull the plug during my trip to the countryside – *Je pourrai enfin me déconnecter pendant mon voyage à la campagne.*

- purchase – *acheter*

She'll purchase more food since Paul and Mary are also invited – *Elle achètera plus de nourriture puisque Paul et Marie sont également invités.*

- pursue – *poursuivre*

I finally decided to pursue my life-long dream and become a scientist – *J'ai enfin décidé de poursuivre le rêve de toute ma vie et de devenir scientifique.*

- put (an object in/on/under something) – *mettre quelque chose dans, sur, en-dessous de quelque chose*

Do you know where I've put my glasses? – *Sais-tu où j'ai mis mes lunettes ?*

- put up with something – *supporter quelque chose*

Because of our new neighbors, we have to put up with screams at night – *A cause de nos nouveaux voisins, il nous faut supporter des cris la nuit.*

- quarrel – *se battre, se disputer*

Children were quarreling down the street and the police had to come and stop them – *Des enfants se battaient / se disputaient en bas de la rue et il a fallu que la police intervienne et les fasse arrêter.*

- sadden – *attrister*

Her death still saddens me very much – *Sa mort m'attriste encore beaucoup.*

- say – *dire, raconter*

What exactly did you say to him? – *Qu'est-ce que tu lui as dit / raconté, exactement ?*

He likes saying nonsense upon meeting new people – *Il aime dire / raconter des bêtises lorsqu'il croise de nouvelles personnes.*

>>> To meet someone spontaneously may also be rendered with *croiser,* in a more idiomatic and relaxed fashion than the traditional *rencontrer / voir.*

- see – *voir*

I can see you behind this fence – *Je peux te voir derrière cette barrière.*

We all saw what happened – *Nous avons tout vu ce qui s'était passé.*

>>> (as an interjection) I see... – *Je vois...*

- sell – *vendre*

    I sold my old car last week – *J'ai vendu ma vieille voiture la semaine dernière.*

- set a record – *établir un record*

    He has set a new record – *Il a établi un nouveau record.*

- set in – *s'installer*

    Fear had suddenly set in their minds – *La peur s'était soudainement installée dans leur esprit.*

- set the record straight – *mettre les points sur les "I" / rétablir les faits*

    I'll set the record straight… – *Je vais mettre les points sur les "I"* ("I'll dot my 'i's'", literally) / *Je vais rétablir les faits.*

- set the table – *mettre la table*

    Come here and set the table – *Viens ici et mets la table.*

- settle (move to a new place) – *s'installer*

    Now that you've settled here, is there anything you would like? – *Maintenant que vous vous êtes installé, y a-t-il quelque chose que vous aimeriez ?*

- should – *devoir*, in the conditional mood (*je devrais, tu devrais, il devrait, nous devrions, vous devriez, ils devraient*)

    You should lock the door once you leave the house – *Tu devrais fermer la porte à clé dès que tu sors de la maison.*

- show – *montrer*

    She showed us her book collection – *Elle nous a montré sa collection de livres.*

- sit down – *s'asseoir*

    He suddenly interrupted his speech and sat down – *Il interrompit son discours soudainement et s'assit.*

- stand up – *se lever*

    As the director entered the room, the pupils stood up – *Tandis que le directeur rentrait dans la pièce, les élèves se levèrent.*

- sleep – *dormir*

    He slept for fourteen consecutive hours – *Il a dormi pendant quatorze heures consécutives.*

- smile – *sourire*

    The cashier smiled at me – *Le caissier m'a souri.*

- speak – *parler, dire*

    I can speak five different languages – *Je peux parler cinq langues différentes.*

    Speak the truth now! – *Dis la vérité maintenant !*

- spend (money) – *dépenser*

    He spent 30€ on his plane ticket – *Il a dépensé 30€ sur son billet d'avion.*

- spend time – *passer du temps*

    I'll take advantage of my Friday to spend time with the kids – *Je profiterai de mon vendredi pour passer du temps avec les enfants.*

- start – *commencer, débuter*

    The film will start soon – *Le film va bientôt débuter / commencer.*

- state (in speech) – *affirmer*

    He stated he had never been there before, but the footage incriminated him – *Il a affirmé qu'il n'était jamais allé là-bas auparavant, mais les images de surveillance l'ont incriminé / ont prouvé sa culpabilité.*

>>> footage (in an investigation) – *des images de surveillance, une bande de surveillance.*

- stop – *arrêter*

    Stop talking to me like this! – *Arrête de me parler comme ça !*

    He suddenly stopped in the middle of the road – *Il s'est soudainement arrêté au milieu de la route.*

- study – *étudier*

    I'll study this plan over the weekend and tell you what I think – *J'étudierai ce plan pendant le week-end et je dirai ce que je pense.*

    She studied hard for her exam – *Elle a beaucoup étudié pour son examen.*

- submit – *soumettre*

    You know what? I'll just submit my application and see what comes out of it – *Tu sais quoi ? Je vais simplement soumettre ma candidature et voir ce qui en résulte.*

    >>> an application (vacancy, school) – *une candidature.*

    >>> what comes out of it – *ce qui en résulte, ce qui en ressort.*

- succeed – *réussir*

    He was never one to succeed without telling people about it – *Il n'était jamais le genre à réussir sans en parler.*

    I'm sure that this time, I'll succeed – *Je suis sûr que cette fois, je réussirai.*

    The woman succeeded in renovating the house within schedule – *La femme a réussi à rénover la maison dans le temps imparti.*

>>> within schedule, within the timeframe – *dans le temps imparti, dans les délais prévus.*

>>> Attention: *un délai* in French is not "a delay", but instead "a deadline"; to have been delayed would however be *être en retard, avoir été retardé.*

- suffer – *souffrir*

    We found a wounded cat by the side of the road; I couldn't let that poor thing suffer – *Nous avons trouvé un chat blessé sur le côté de la route ; je ne pouvais pas laisser ce pauvre animal souffrir.*

    And he just told us: "Make them suffer!" – *Et il nous a simplement dit : « Faites-les souffrir ! »*

- support (financially, emotionally, logically) – *soutenir*

    The widow was glad so many people supported her during these tragic events – *La veuve était heureuse que tant de personnes l'aient soutenue pendant ces événements tragiques.*

    >>> an event – *un événement.*

    >>> so many people – *tant de personnes, tant de gens.*

- suppose – *supposer*

    Should I suppose you disobeyed my orders once again? – *Dois-je supposer que tu as désobéi à mes ordres une fois de plus ?*

    I suppose he'll be here soon – *Je suppose qu'il sera là bientôt.*

- take (away from; seize) – *prendre*

    Do take your coat with you, it's cold outside – *Prends bien ton manteau avec toi, il fait froid dehors.*

    Take what you want – *Prends ce que tu veux.*

He won't take my pride away from me – *Il ne me prendra pas ma fierté.*

- take (time; to last) – *prendre*

    It should take us thirty minutes at most – *Cela devrait nous prendre trente minutes tout au plus.*

- take on (try) – *se mettre à*

    He took on woodworking since he was bored on the weekends – *Il s'est mis à la menuiserie comme il s'ennuyé le week-end.*

- talk – *parler*

    We talked about our lives in a nearby café – *Nous avons parlé de nos vies dans un café à proximité.*

- tell – *dire*

    Just tell him how you feel! – *Dis-lui simplement ce que tu ressens !*

- tell (ie I can't tell which one is which) – *dire, deviner*

    Could you tell who's older? – *Pourrais-tu dire / Pourrais-tu deviner qui est le plus vieux ?*

- think – *penser, se dire*

    I was thinking… When will they leave? – *Je me disais… Quand est-ce qu'ils vont partir ?*

    She thought the library would still be open – *Elle pensait que la bibliothèque serait toujours ouverte.*

- trust – *faire confiance à*

    Do you trust me? – *Me fais-tu confiance ?*

- try – *essayer*

Try eating more vegetables if you want to lose weight – *Essaye de manger plus de légumes si tu veux perdre du poids.*

- understand – *comprendre*

I understand now: we shouldn't have taken that decision – *Je comprends maintenant : nous n'aurions pas dû prendre cette décision.*

- wait – *attendre*

You've only got to wait: there will be something better around the corner – *Il faut juste que tu attendes : tu trouveras bientôt quelque chose de mieux.*

- walk – *marcher*

He walked in a puddle of water – *Il marcha dans une flaque d'eau.*

- wander – *se promener* (wandering intently), *errer* (can be intently or not), *flâner*

He was wandering in the forest when I found him – *Il était en train de se promener dans la forêt quand je l'ai trouvé.* (i.e. He was walking in the forest) / *Il errait dans la forêt quand je l'ai trouvé.* (denotes aimlessness) / *Il flânait* (wandered aimlessly) …

- want – *vouloir*

What do you want for breakfast? – *Qu'est-ce que tu veux pour le petit-déjeuner ?*

I want him to be more disciplined – *Je veux qu'il soit plus discipliné.*

- win – *gagner*

They swore they would win – *Ils ont assuré qu'ils allaient gagner.*

- wipe off – *essuyer*

    He wiped sweat off his forehead – *Il essuya la transpiration de son front.*

- wish – *désirer ; aimer tellement* – in the conditional (*j'aimerais...*)

    I wish you were here – *J'aimerais que tu sois là.* (*désirer* wouldn't really work here)

    I wish to order... – *Je désire commander / J'aimerais commander...*

- wonder – *se demander*

    I was wondering when the last time we went on holidays was – *Je me demandais quand était la dernière fois que nous sommes allés en vacances.*

- work – *travailler*

    He likes working so much he doesn't even come back home – *Il aime tellement travailler qu'il ne revient pas à la maison.*

- work overtime – *faire des heures supplémentaires /* (colloquial) *faire des heures sup'*

    I need a bit more money, so I'll be working overtime at the end of the week – *J'ai besoin d'un peu plus d'argent, donc je ferai des heures supplémentaires à la fin de la semaine.*

- work wonders – *faire des merveilles, faire des miracles*

    Moving to another country has worked wonders on his mental state – *S'installer à l'étranger a fait des merveilles pour son état mental.*

    >>> get behind in your work – *être en retard sur son travail.*

    Despite supervising him regularly, he's still behind on his work – *Malgré le fait que je le supervise régulièrement, il est toujours en retard sur son travail.*

- work off – (one's energy) *dépenser son énergie ;* (one's anger) *éliminer sa colère, tempérer sa colère*

> She went for a walk because she needed to work off her anger – *Elle est allée faire un tour parce qu'elle avait besoin d'éliminer sa colère.*

- work one's ass off – *se tuer à la tâche, s'évertuer* (both idioms)

> She's the kind of girl who's always working her ass off for her friends – *C'est le type de fille qui s'évertue tout le temps / se tue tout le temps à la tâche pour ses amis.*

- work oneself into the ground – *se tuer à la tâche*
- work (of a machine, concept) – *fonctionner, marcher*

> Their social media strategy definitely worked well – *Leur stratégie sur les réseaux sociaux a définitivement bien marché.*

- stop working (of a person) – *arrêter de travailler*
- stop working (of a machine) – *cesser de fonctionner* (quite formal, only for apps, machinery, and computer programs) / *s'être arrêté* (temporarily – literally "has stopped") / *ne plus marcher* (won't work at all anymore; commonly used for items and machinery)

> Windows has stopped working – *Windows a cessé de fonctionner.*

> You hadn't told me the television had stopped working – *Tu ne m'avais pas dit que la télévision s'était arrêtée ! / ne marchait plus !*

- worry – *s'inquiéter*

> Don't worry, we've worked enough for today – *Ne t'inquiète pas, nous avons assez travaillé pour aujourd'hui.*

> >>> Also note: I'm worried he won't listen to me – *J'ai peur qu'il ne veuille pas m'écouter. (j'ai peur que + subjunctive).*

- would – a verb with *would* is conjugated in the conditional mood:

> I would like a Diet Coke and a bag of crisps, please – *J'aimerais un Coca Light et un sachet de chips, s'il vous plaît.*

Chapter 7 – Buying Things and Paying

- to buy – *acheter*

- a purchase – *un achat*

> I've got to make a couple of purchases in town – *J'ai besoin de faire quelques achats en ville.*

- to sell – *vendre*

- a sale – *une vente*

- a cost, a price – *un prix*

- a price tag – *une étiquette*

> I didn't see any price tag on this jacket – *Je n'ai pas vu d'étiquette sur cette veste.*

- to cost – *coûter*

> How much will this cost me? – *Combien est-ce que ça va me coûter ?*

- a credit – *un crédit*

- on credit – *à crédit*

- a wallet – *un porte-feuille, un porte-monnaie*

- to steal – *voler*

- a five-finger discount – i.e. I got a five-finger discount on this scarf – *J'ai eu cette écharpe en la volant / J'ai volé cette écharpe* (French doesn't have an adequate idiom to translate the English – in French, both sentences would mean *stealing* – a better translation would be, *J'ai eu une super reduction sur cette écharpe, c'était presque du vol* ; the price was so low that it felt like stealing)

- supplies – *des marchandises*

- an item – *un objet*

- in bulk – *en gros*

> I prefer to buy packs of bottles of water in bulk – *Je préfère acheter des packs de bouteilles d'eau en gros.*

- a discount – *une réduction*

- 10 / 20 / 30% off – *réduction de 10 / 20 / 30%*

- a receipt – *une facture, un reçu*

> Could I have a receipt, please? – *Pourrais-je avoir un reçu / une facture, s'il vous plaît ?*

- change – *la monnaie*

> Here's the change – *Voici la monnaie.*
>
> Do you have any spare change? – *Avez-vous un peu de monnaie ? / Avez-vous de la monnaie en trop ?*

- an invoice – *une facture*

- a bank – *une banque*

- a branch – *une banque*

> Could you tell me where the nearest branch is? – *Pourriez-vous me dire où se trouve la banque la plus proche ?*

- a transfer – *un virement*

- an ATM – *un distributeur, un distributeur de billets*

- to withdraw banknotes – *retirer des billets*

    >>> banknotes, notes – *des billets* (I found a ten-dollar note on the ground – *J'ai trouvé un billet de dix dollars sur le sol*).

- a credit card – *une carte de crédit, une carte bleue, une CB, une carte* (from least to most used)

- by card – *par carte, en CB* (abbreviation of *carte bleue*), *en carte bleue*

    May I pay by card? – *Pourrais-je payer par carte / en CB / en carte bleue ?*

- by chèque – *en chèque*

- by cash – *en espèces*

- coins – *des pièces*

    I've got many coins to trade – *J'ai beaucoup de pièces à échanger.*

- a shop, a store – *un magasin, une boutique*

    I saw a couple of interesting stores on the way home, I'll give them a look – *J'ai vu quelques boutiques intéressantes en rentrant à la maison, j'y jeterai un coup d'œil.*

    >>> to give something a look – *jeter un coup d'oeil à quelque chose.*

- a transaction – *une transaction*

- a checkout – *une caisse*

    Please proceed to the checkout – *Veuillez-vous avancer vers la caisse.*

    >>> to proceed (move towards) – *s'avancer.*

- an employee – *un(e) employé(e)*

- a cashier – *un caissier, une caissière*

- waiting in line – *une file d'attente*

- to stand in line – *se tenir en file indienne*

>   Everybody was standing in line as the shop opened – *Tout le monde se tenait en file indienne lorsque la boutique ouvrit.*

>   \>>> to open (of a shop) – *ouvrir, être ouvert.*

Chapter 8 – Numbers and the Hour

Numbers:

one – *un, une* (depending on the gender)

I saw an abandoned bike near the railroad – *J'ai vu une bicyclette abandonnée / un vélo abandonné près de la voie ferrée.*

two – *deux*

three – *trois*

four – *quatre*

five – *cinq*

six – *six*

seven – *sept*

eight – *huit*

nine – *neuf*

ten – *dix*

eleven – *onze*

twelve – *douze*

thirteen – *treize*

fourteen – *quatorze*

fifteen – *quinze*

sixteen – *seize*

seventeen – *dix-sept*

eighteen – *dix-huit*

nineteen – *dix-neuf*

All two-number digits after twenty (*vingt*) follow either one of two patterns:

1. twenty-one, twenty-two, twenty-three: French also commonly appends both digits together, with the exception of some ending with "one" where *et* is added: *vingt-et-un, trente-et-un…*

2. Exceptions: a few numbers, instead of being followed by "one", "two"… are followed by "eleven", "twelve"… They are: *seventy* and its compounds (*soixante-dix, soixante-et-onze, soixante-douze…*) and *ninety* (*quatre-vingt-onze, quatre-vingt-douze…*)

A notable phenomenon is that "eighty" is literally translated as "four-twenty", hence *quatre-vingt-un* ("eighty-one") and *quatre-vingt-onze* ("ninety one", or "four-twenty-eleven").

For each of those numbers, you'll have the first four to help you know which variant to use:

Twenty – *vingt*

Twenty-one – *vingt-et-un*

Twenty-two – *vingt-deux*

Twenty-three – *vingt-trois*

Thirty – *trente*

Thirty-one – *trente-et-un*

Thirty-two – *trente-deux*

Thirty-three – *trente-trois*

Forty – *quarante*

Forty-one – *quarante-et-un*

Forty-two – *quarante-deux*

Forty-three – *quarante-trois*

Fifty – *cinquante*

Fifty-one – *cinquante-et-un*

Fifty-two – *cinquante-deux*

Fifty-three – *cinquante-trois*

Sixty – *soixante*

Sixty-one – *soixante-et-un*

Sixty-two – *soixante-deux*

Sixty-three – *soixante-trois*

Seventy – *soixante-dix*

Seventy-one – *soixante-et-onze*

Seventy-two – *soixante-douze*

Seventy-three – *soixante-treize*

Eighty – *quatre-vingt*

Eighty-one – *quatre-vingt-un*

Eighty-two – *quatre-vingt-deux*

Eighty-three – *quatre-vingt-trois*

Ninety – *quatre-vingt-dix*

Ninety-one – *quatre-vingt-onze*

Ninety-two – *quatre-vingt-douze*

Ninety-three – *quatre-vingt-treize*

One hundred – *cent*

Two hundred – *deux cents*

Three hundred – *trois cents*

One thousand, two thousand – *un millier / mille* (*mille* is much more common), *deux milles*

> One thousand activists gathered up near the town hall – *Un millier de militants / Mille militants se sont rassemblés près de la mairie.*

One million, two million – *un million, deux millions*

Tell the hour:

- a clock – *une horloge*

- a watch – *une montre*

- a hand (of a clock) – *une aiguille* (minute hand: *grande aiguille*; second hand: *petite aiguille / la trotteuse*)

- a delay – *un retard*

- to arrive in advance – *arriver en avance*

- to anticipate, plan – *prévoir, anticiper*

- What time is it? – *Quelle heure est-il?*

- It's three AM – *Il est trois heures du matin.*

- It's nine o'clock – *Il est neuf heures pile / neuf heures.*

> >>> o'clock – *pile*, not translated (you'd only add *pile* if you want to emphasize that the clock has really just struck 9 AM or PM).

- It's noon – *Il est midi.*

- It's a quarter past seven – *Il est sept heures et quart.*

- It's a quarter to eight – *Il est huit heures moins le quart / Il est sept heures quarante-cinq* (7:45)

>>> a quarter past… – *et quart.*

>>> a quarter to… – hour to come (8:00 here) + *moins le quart* ; previous hour (7:00) + *quarante-cinq.*

- It's three to four – *Il est trois heures cinquante-sept.*

>>> When there is such a negligible number of minutes to reach an hour, French will privilege the whole number of minutes out of sixty.

- It's 10:24 PM – *Il est 10 heures 24.* (no *et* is included either between the hour and the minutes)

- He should come back at around 11:30 – *Il devrait revenir aux alentours de onze heures trente.*

>>> at around (an hour) – *aux alentours de…*

>>> near (a place), nearby – *aux alentours de…* (St-Laurent-du-Var is a city near Nice – *… est une ville près de Nice / aux alentours de Nice.*)

- I can only fall asleep after midnight – *Je ne peux m'endormir qu'après minuit.*

Chapter 9 – Arguing: Common Verbs and Nouns

- to be right – *avoir raison*

- to be wrong, to err – *avoir tort, se tromper*

- to know – *savoir*

    I know what I saw! – *Je sais que ce j'ai vu !*

- to tell – *dire*

    Perhaps you can tell us what all of this is about – *Vous pouvez / Tu peux peut-être nous dire ce qui se passe exactement ?*

- to explain – *expliquer*

    There's not much to explain, really… – *Il n'y a pas grand-chose à expliquer, vraiment…*

- to argue – (put forth an argument) *argumenter* ; (strife with someone) *se disputer avec…*

    I won't argue with you anymore, it gets on my nerves – *J'arrête de me disputer avec toi, ça me tape sur les nerfs.*

- to defend – *défendre*

    I think he has a position to defend – *Je pense qu'il a une position à défendre.*

- to think – *penser*

    I think he's making a big mistake, but of course he won't listen to me – *Je pense qu'il est en train de faire une grosse bêtise, mais évidemment il ne veut pas m'écouter.*

    >>> a mistake – *une erreur* (quite formal), *une bêtise*

    I was thinking about buying a new car, what do you think of it? – *J'étais en train de penser à acheter une nouvelle voiture, qu'est-ce que tu en penses ?*

- it seems to (me, you…) that – *il (me, te…) semble que*

    It seems to me that we shouldn't be here – *Il me semble qu'on ne devrait pas être là.*

- to be under the impression that – *avoir l'impression que…*

    She was under the impression that it had all been a hoax, but we cast out her doubts – *Elle avait l'impression que tout cela n'avait été qu'un canular, mais nous avons dissipé ses doutes.*

- a point of view – *un point de vue*

    We sure have many diverse points of view tonight… – *Nous avons de toute évidence beaucoup de points de vue variés ce soir…*

- an idea – *une idée*

- an opinion – *une opinion, un avis*

    What's your opinion about the upcoming debate? – *Quelle est ton/votre opinion / ton/votre avis par rapport au prochain débat / débat qui arrive ?*

- an innovation – *une innovation*

- a fallacy – *un erreur, une idée fausse* ; (to be a fallacy) *être erroné, caduque*

> Your argument is an obvious fallacy since you didn't bother to answer most of my questions – *Ton / Votre argument est de toute évidence erroné / caduque puisque vous ne vous êtes pas donné la peine de répondre à la plupart de mes questions.*

- an invention – *une invention*

- a story – *une histoire*

- I think (that)… – *Je pense que* (*que* is always compulsory in French, whereas *that* can be omitted)

> I think your new exercise regimen will work well in the following weeks – *Je pense que ton nouveau régime d'exercices fonctionnera bien dans les prochaines semaines.*

- According to… – *Selon…*

> According to sources close to the victim… – *Selon des sources proches de la victime…*

> Well, according to this website, eating sugar is not harmful in small quantities – *Et bien, selon ce site Internet, manger du sucre n'est pas nocif en petites quantités.*

- After all… – *Après tout…*

- I beg to differ – *Permets-moi / Permettez-moi de ne pas être d'accord*

- Well… – *Eh/Et bien…*

Structuring your argument and explaining cause and consequence:

Apart from specialized textbooks aimed at university students or people preparing for exams and certifications, it's often pretty hard to find sentences to express your opinions and put forth arguments –

which is why we have created this section for you to shine, both when writing and speaking French!

- first of all – *dans un premier temps, d'abord*

> First of all, the numbers are wrong – *Dans un premier temps / D'abord, les chiffres sont erronés.*
>
> >>> wrong (erroneous, nonfactual) – *erroné* (using *faux* would be confusing since it can also be "forged", as in "That painting is forged", or "tampered", as in "Somebody tampered with the numbers").

- then – *ensuite* (chronologically or argumentatively); *dans un second temps* (when presenting an argument)

> I then designed a plan to reach that goal – *J'ai ensuite conçu un plan pour atteindre cet objectif.*

- finally – *enfin*

> Finally, I think you ought to take care of your finances – *Enfin, je pense que tu te dois de prendre soin de tes finances. / tu dois prendre soin de tes finances.*

- ought to – *se devoir de faire quelque chose, devoir faire quelque chose*

> He ought to extend a hand to everyone in the country – *Il doit tendre la main à tous ses concitoyens.*
>
> >>> inhabitants in the same country as you – *concitoyens*, from *un citoyen* – a citizen.
>
> >>> extend a hand, lend a helping hand – *aider, tendre la main.*

- must – *devoir faire quelque chose*

> But surely there must be something that the government can do – *Mais il doit sûrement y avoir quelque chose que le gouvernement peut faire.*

- I would first like to introduce… – *J'aimerais d'abord introduire… / présenter*

    I would first like to introduce the fact that none of them attended the party – *J'aimerais d'abord introduire le fait / présenter le fait qu'aucun d'entre eux n'était à la fête.*

    >>> to attend a party, a ceremony – *être (présent) à une fête, à une cérémonie.*

- on one hand, on the other hand – *d'une part, d'autre part*

    On the one hand, he was terribly nice to us – *D'une part, il s'est montré extrêmement gentil envers nous.*

    >>> to be nice to someone – *être gentil envers quelqu'un, se montrer gentil envers quelqu'un.*

- but what about…? – *mais qu'en est-il de… / du… / de la… ?*

    But what about the new highway that was built just behind the house? – *Mais qu'en est-il de la nouvelle autoroute qui a été construite juste derrière la maison ?*

    >>> the highway – *l'autoroute.*

- yet – *cependant*

    He seems nice enough, yet I can't bring myself to trust him – *Il a l'air plutôt gentil, cependant je ne parviens pas à lui faire confiance.*

    >>> to trust someone – *faire confiance à quelqu'un.*

- although – *même si* + indicative verb, *bien que* + subjunctive verb

    Of course you're right, although I should add that… – *Bien sûr que tu as raison, même si je devrais ajouter que… / bien que je doive ajouter que…*

- because – *parce que, car* (you'll see *car* used in oral speech more often than not, since it's much shorter than *parce que*)

We couldn't afford to hire anybody because we had already gone over budget – *Nous ne pouvions pas nous permettre d'embaucher quelqu'un parce que nous avions déjà dépassé notre budget.*

- since (causal) – *puisque*

    Since no one bothered to do it, I'll take care of it myself – *Puisque personne ne s'est donné la peine de le faire, je m'en chargerai moi-même.*

- I believe this was caused by… – *Je pense que ça a été causé par…*

- What actually happened is that… – *Ce qui s'est en fait passé, c'est que…*

- What will come out of it? – *Qu'est-ce qui en résultera ?*

- I think consequences will be dire – *Je pense que les conséquences seront terribles.*

- I strongly believe that… – *Je crois fermement que / J'ai l'intime conviction que…*

- I had never thought of that possibility – *Je n'avais jamais pensé à cette possibilité.*

- The root of the problem is quite simple, really – *La source / racine du problème est assez simple en vérité.*

- We've got to get to the bottom of it – *Il faut que nous fassions la lumière là-dessus*

    >>> go to the bottom of a problem – *faire la lumière sur…* (shed light on, literally)

- to prompt someone to – *inciter quelqu'un à*

    That event prompted him to adopt a wholly different strategy – *Cet événement l'a incité à adopter une stratégie totalement différente.*

- to force someone to, coerce someone into – *forcer quelqu'un à*

Recent riots forced him to reconsider his position and change his tactics – *Des manifestations récentes l'ont forcé à reconsidérer sa position et à changer de tactique.*

>>> change one's tactics – *changer sa tactique, changer de tactique* (the word almost always remains in the singular in French).

- That idea planted the seed for a whole new strategy – *Cette idée a fait germer l'idée d'une toute nouvelle stratégie.*

>>> plant the seed for, foster – *faire germer l'idée.*

Chapter 10 – Informal Speech / Interjections

What most learners rightfully view as their struggling point when it comes to delving deeper into a language, is mastering conversations, and the occasional informal sentence. Indeed, few people speak French like 19th-century aristocrats! That's why we have compiled here not only common interjections to pepper throughout your conversations, but also more informal expressions. There is a whole system of French in its own right too: *le verlan*, which we'll briefly touch upon. *Le verlan* is predominantly informal and consists of inversing syllables in a given word. Sometimes, it simply marks informal speech, while it can directly change the word's meaning in other occasions – for example, to say that something is "crazy" can be either *fou* or *ouf* (both meanings are the same), while *méchant* (nasty) turns into *chanmé* (excellent or sick, as in "Man, that song is sick!"). It is admittedly mostly used by young children and adolescents, but adding some more flavor to your style or simply being able to recognize these quirks when they are used can definitely come in handy!

Please note that since most of these expressions are slang or used in rather informal conversations, you'll encounter many instances when the negative particle *ne* won't be present.

- Go ahead; help yourself – *Fais-toi plaisir, fais comme chez toi*

> Can I borrow some of these pens? – Go ahead. – *Est-ce que je peux t'emprunter quelques-uns de ces stylos ? – Fais-toi plaisir / Fais comme chez toi.*

- Sure (when granting a request) – *Bien sûr ; sans souci.*

- No way (when refusing a request) – *Absolument pas.*

- No way! (expressing surprise) – *Sans déconner* (slang, informal) ! / *Tu rigoles ! / Sans blague !* (the last one, while it isn't formal, is really conversational)

- No way he's gonna do it – *Il le fera jamais !* (literally "He'll never do it") / *Il osera pas le faire !*

- No hard feelings – *sans rancune*

- Jesus Christ / Holy cow! – *La vache !*

- It was time – *Il était temps !*

- Nonsense! (when disproving or disbelieving something) – *N'importe quoi !*

- That's crazy! – *C'est fou / ouf !*

- Don't tell me about it! – *M'en parle / parlez pas !*

- You see! ("... I was right; it actually happened") – *Tu vois !*

- Did you see that? – (if it were extremely formal) *As-tu vu ça ? ;* (regular conversation) *Est-ce que tu as vu ça ? ;* (informal) *T'as vu ça ?*

- Drop it! ("... this topic") – *Laisse tomber / bétom !*

- That was so sick! – *C'était trop ouf / C'était chanmé !*

- Cut me some slack! – *Laisse-moi tranquille / Laisse-moi respirer !*

- C'mon! – *Allez !*

- Please! – *s'il te plaît*, often pronounced colloquially as *ste-plaît / s'il vous plaît – s'vous-plaît !*

- Well done! – *Bien joué ! / Respect !*

- Let's go! – *Allons-y ! / C'est parti ! (verlan : C'est ti-par !)*

- Here we go! – *C'est parti !*

- Alright / Fine – *Ok / D'accord.*

- Sounds good – *ça me paraît bien.*

- I'm in – *J'en suis / Allons-y*

- Well well well… – *Tiens tiens tiens… / Tiens donc…*

- Indeed / So it seems – *En effet / On dirait bien.*

- bloke, dude, mate – *mec* (can be used with positive and negative connotations)

> Hey mate, what have you been doing all this time? – *Hé mec, qu'est-ce que tu as fait pendant tout ce temps ?*
>
> Stop looking at me like that, dude! – *Arrête de me regarder comme ça, mec !*

- guy – *mec* (positive), *mec/type* (negative; *type* is always connotated with strange people who may make you uncomfortable)

> So I met that really nice guy a couple of days ago… – *Alors j'ai rencontré ce mec sympa il y a quelques jours…*
>
> Some weird guy was following me the other night – *Un mec/type bizarre m'a suivi la nuit dernière*
>
> What a strange guy! – *Quel type bizarre !*

Note: the *verlan* for *mec* is *keum*, and is mostly used in a humorous way to talk about a ridiculous, preferably young male person.

- girl, lady – *meuf* (verlan for *femme*, a woman; may be used affectionately, but unless you're with friends it's pretty derogatory)

> I'm glad you're doing fine, girl! – *Je suis contente que tout se passe bien pour toi, meuf !*

- a thing – *une chose, un truc*

I found that thing at the bottom of a box – *J'ai trouvé ce truc / cette chose au fond d'une boîte*.

The thing is… – *Le truc, c'est que…* (would always be *truc*).

Overly loud parties are not really my thing – *Les fêtes extrêmement bruyantes sont pas vraiment mon truc* (would always be *truc* as a synonym for "Are not really my cup of tea" – *ne sont pas vraiment ma tasse de thé*).

Chapter 11 – Meeting Someone

For the first time:

- to meet someone (for the first time) – *rencontrer quelqu'un pour la première fois*

> It is nice meeting you! – *C'est un plaisir de te / vous rencontrer !*

- to call (on the phone) – *appeler*

> I'll call you later – *Je t'appellerai plus tard.*

- to talk to, speak with – *parler à...*

- personal information – *des informations personnelles*

- a name – *un nom*

> What's your name? – *Comment tu t'appelles / vous vous appelez ? / Quel est ton / votre nom ?* (much less common than the first possibility). In a rather formal context, you can use instead: *Comment t'appelles-tu ? / Comment vous appelez-vous ?*

- an age – *un âge*

What's your age? – *Quel est ton / votre âge ?*

- a (phone) number – *un numéro (de téléphone)*

- an address – *une adresse*

May I get your phone number? Your address, maybe? – *Est-ce que je peux avoir ton / votre numéro (de téléphone) ? Ton / Votre adresse, peut-être ?*

- personality traits – *des traits de personnalité / traits de caractère* (more used)

- to come from a country, a city – *venir d'un pays, d'une ville*

- place of origin – *endroit d'où (je, tu, il...) + "venir"* (to come, conjugated present tense).

My place of origin is in Greece – *L'endroit d'où je viens, c'est la Grèce.*

- city, country, region of origin – *ville, pays, région natal(e)* ("of birth")

Where do you come from? – I come from London, and you? – *D'où viens-tu / venez-vous ? Je viens de Londres, et toi / et vous ?*

So, what's your country of origin? – *Alors, quel est ton pays natal ?*

- to be (reside, travel, stand) somewhere – *être quelque part*

How long have you been here? – *Depuis combien de temps es-tu / êtes-vous ici ?*

Asking more questions:

- So, tell me more about yourself – *Alors, dis-m'en plus sur toi / dites-m'en plus sur vous.*

- What do I need to know about you? – *Qu'est-ce que j'ai besoin de savoir sur vous / toi ?*

- a job – *un travail*

> What is your current job? – *Quel est ton travail en ce moment ?* ("current" may also be *actuel*, but less frequently so).

- a craft (i.e. a job) – *un métier*

> My craft is pretty specialized; let me tell you more about it... - *Mon métier est plutôt spécialisé ; laisse-moi t'en dire plus...*

- responsibilities - *responsabilités*

> Can you tell me more about your responsibilities? – *Peux-tu / Pouvez-vous m'en dire plus sur tes / vos responsabilités ?*

- to like something about – *aimer quelque chose dans un film, livre, travail ; aimer quelque chose chez quelqu'un*

> What do you like (most) about your job? – *Qu'est-ce que tu aimes (le plus) dans ton travail.*

- to like, enjoy doing something – *aimer faire quelque chose* (only *'aimer'* is conjugated in a sentence)

> I like knitting and reading the newspaper – *J'aime tricoter et lire le journal.*

- I'm not a big fan of watching movies – *Ce n'est pas trop mon truc de regarder des films.*

- a hobby – *un hobby, un passe-temps* (invariable in the plural)

> What are your hobbies? – Well, I like reading in my spare time... – *Quels sont tes hobbies / passe-temps ? – Et bien, j'aime lire pendant mon temps libre.*

> >>> in one's spare time – *pendant / dans mon, ton... temps libre.*

- a passion – *une passion*

You must have many passions, right? – *Tu dois avoir de nombreuses passions, pas vrai ?*

- to be passionate about – *être passionné de / par*

I've always been passionate about collecting old car models; what about you? – *J'ai toujours été passionnée par la collection de vieux modèles de voitures ; et toi ?*

- to be interested in something – *être intéressé(e) par quelque chose*

What interests you the most here? – *Qu'est-ce qui t'intéresse le plus ici ?*

What are your main interests? – *Qu'est-ce qui t'intéresse principalement / le plus ?*

>>> Keeping the sentence centered around the verb "to interest" sounds more fluent in French.

Keeping in touch:

- keep in touch – *rester en contact*

Let's keep in touch! – *Restons en contact !*

Due to my relocation, I won't be able to keep in touch with you – *A cause de mon déménagement, je ne pourrai pas rester en contact avec toi / vous.*

- by e-mail, text messages – *par e-mail, SMS*

- to hear from someone – *avoir des nouvelles de quelqu'un*

You'll definitely hear from me soon! – *Tu auras certainement des nouvelles de moi bientôt !*

- to reach (contact) someone – *joindre quelqu'un*

Give me your number so that I may reach you – *Donne-moi ton numéro pour que je puisse te joindre.*

- See you later! / See you soon! – *On se voit plus tard !* (informal) / *A plus tard* (usable in all contexts) !

- Bye! – *Bye bye !*

- to hear from someone (get news) – *avoir des nouvelles de quelqu'un*

>I hope to hear from you soon! – *J'espère avoir de tes / vos nouvelles bientôt !*

Asking for updates:

- Everything's fine for you? - *Tout va bien pour toi ?*

- So, how's everything going? – *Alors, comment ça se passe ?*

- How are you doing? – *Comment ça va / vas-tu / allez-vous ?*

- How have you been since last time? – *Comment ça va depuis la dernière fois ?*

- Got any good news for me / to tell me? – *Tu as des bonnes nouvelles pour moi / à me dire ?*

- It's fine – *ça va*

- Meh… – *On fait aller…*

- It's all been great for me – *Tout s'est très bien passé pour moi.*

>>>> In French, *tout se passe bien* literally means "everything's going fine". It's very commonly used when you want to summarize what's been going on with your life or how you feel about a particular thing.

- Everybody's great – *Tout le monde va bien.*

- I've got to tell you about this new thing – *Il faut que je te parle de ce nouveau truc.*

>>>> A "thing" in French may be *chose* or *truc*: the latter has become very common when talking about events or items, whereas *chose* has become slightly derogatory (i.e. What is that thing?? – *Qu'est-ce que c'est que cette chose ??*)

- In fact, I'm planning to… – *En fait, j'ai prévu de…* (past conjugation in the *passé composé*).

Chapter 12 – Scheduling a Get-Together:

- to schedule – *planifier, prévoir*

    We'll have to schedule something – *Il va falloir qu'on prévoit / planifie quelque chose.*

- to go somewhere – *aller quelque part (*go to... – *aller à)*

    Why don't we go to the cinema next time? – *Pourquoi est-ce qu'on n'irait pas au cinéma la prochaine fois ?*

- to meet (again) – *se voir*

    We should meet again one of these days – *On devrait se voir un de ces jours.*

- When and where will we meet next time? – *Quand et où on se verra la prochaine fois ?*

In town – at the local theater / cinema:

- a ticket – *un billet*

- a new release – *un nouveau film*

- a discount – *une réduction*
- a movie, a film – *un film*
- a plot – *un scénario*

  I found the plot a bit lukewarm, didn't you? – *J'ai trouvé le scénario un peu ennuyeux, et toi ?*

- a character – *une personne*
- a setting – *un environnement, un endroit*

  The main setting during the whole movie was an old barn – *L'endroit principal pendant toute la durée du film était une vieille grange.*

In town – eating out:

- a restaurant – *un restaurant*
- food – *de la nourriture*

  What kind of food do you prefer? – *Quel type de nourriture préfères-tu / préférez-vous ?*

- vegetarian / vegan – *végétarien(ne), végan(e)*
- an allergy – *une allergie*
- allergic – *être allergique*

  Are you allergic to anything, just to be sure? – *Tu es / Vous êtes allergique à quelque chose, juste pour êtes sûr ?*

- a menu – *un menu, une carte*

  Anything spark your interest on the menu? – *Il y a quelque chose qui t'intéresse sur le menu ?*

- a napkin – *une serviette*
- a serving, a portion – *une portion*
- a second helping – *un deuxième service, une deuxième portion*

I'll have a second helping – *Je prendrai une deuxième portion.*

- a buffet – *un buffet*

- an all you can eat buffet – *un buffet à volonté*

- have dinner – *aller dîner* ("to go dine", literally)

We'll have dinner tomorrow – *Nous irons dîner demain.*

- go get lunch – *sortir déjeuner* ("go have lunch outside", literally)

We also could go get lunch – *Nous pourrions aussi sortir déjeuner.*

- get a drink – *aller boire quelque chose* (formal); *prendre un verre, boire un verre* (both slightly informal), *boire un coup* (very informal)

Me and my friends went for a drink in town yesterday evening – *Moi et mes amis sommes allés prendre un verre / boire un coup en ville hier soir.*

>>> in town – *en ville.*

- grab a bite – *(aller) manger un morceau*

I could grab a bite before coming home – *Je pourrais (aller) manger un morceau avant de rentrer à la maison.*

>>> come (back) home – *rentrer à la maison.*

- a booking – *une réservation*

I'll make a booking for four – *Je ferai une réservation pour quatre.*

- It's on the house – *C'est la maison qui paye.*

- the bill – *l'addition*

- to split the bill – *séparer l'addition*

I agree, but we'll have to split the bill – *Je suis d'accord, mais on devra séparer l'addition.*

- I really enjoyed our dinner – *J'ai vraiment aimé notre dîner.*

- That breakfast was absolutely delicious – *Ce petit-déjeuner était absolument délicieux.*

- We definitely should come back here sometime – *On devrait définitivement revenir par ici un de ces jours.*

>>> idiom: "Come back here" – *revenir par ici, revenir ici.*

>>> sometime – *un de ces jours, un de ces quatre* (more informal).

- It was nice going out – *C'était cool / bien de sortir.*

- We should do it again next week – *On devrait remettre ça* (fixed expression) *la semaine prochaine.*

>>> do something again – *remettre ça.*

- Let's do it again soon – *Remettons-ça bientôt !*

About scheduling a meet-up:

- to be available – *être disponible, dispo* (more common), *libre*

I'll only be available on the weekends – *Je ne serai dispo / libre que les week-ends.*

When are you available next week? – *Quand es-tu disponible la semaine prochaine ?*

- to accommodate someone – *avoir du temps pour quelqu'un / pour voir quelqu'un*

Can you accommodate me on July 27th? – *Est-ce que vous aurez / tu auras du temps pour me voir le 27 juillet ?*

- have enough time – *avoir assez de temps*

- carve out some time – *se libérer* (pronominal verb, works on its own in a sentence), *prendre du temps libre*

Perhaps I'll be able to carve out some time for you – *Peut-être que j'arriverai à me libérer pour toi / prendre du temps libre pour toi.*

>>> be able to do something – *arriver à faire quelque chose.*

- to be there (having just arrived) – *être là, y être* (can be used for past, present or future encounters), *être arrivé* (preferably in the past)

Sure, I'll be there – *Bien sûr, je serai là / j'y serai.*

I'm there – *Je suis là / J'y suis / Je suis arrivé(e).*

- I'm so sorry, something came up at the last minute – *Je suis vraiment désolée, j'ai eu un empêchement de dernière minute.* (The French customarily say "I got a last-minute impediment", contrary to English which puts more emphasis on the impediment itself.)

>>> impediment (unexpected event that troubles your plans) – *empêchement.*

>>> last-minute (call, break, etc.) – *de dernière minute* (fixed expression).

- If you're so busy, we should probably reschedule – *Si tu es / vous êtes si occupé(e), nous devrions peut-être reporter notre rendez-vous / déjeuner...*

>>> It is almost compulsory to add which event is being rescheduled in French, i.e. a meeting, lunch break, appointment... while English doesn't need it.

Chapter 13 – Traveling:

Being on the way:

- a route – *une route, un itinéraire*

> What would be the most efficient route to get to the nearest hotel? – *Que serait la route / l'itinéraire le plus efficace pour aller jusqu'à l'hôtel le plus proche ?*

- a map – *une carte*

> We've fortunately brought some maps to help us get a better sense of the place – *Heureusement, nous avons amenés des cartes pour nous aider à mieux appréhender l'endroit.*
>
> >>> to get a better sense of… – *mieux appréhender…*

- an itinerary – *un itinéraire*

> So, having planned the itinerary from point A to point B… – *Donc, comme nous avons planifié un itinéraire du point A au point B…*

- a destination – *une destination*

Our next destination shall be the Taj Mahal – *Notre prochaine destination sera le Taj Mahal.*

- a shortcut – *un raccourci*

    Many natives graciously showed us shortcuts around the town – *Beaucoup d'autochtones nous ont gracieusement montré des raccourcis à divers endroits en ville.*

- a distance – *une distance*

    Sure, the distance was a deterrent, but we ended up enjoying our trip so much – *Bien sûr, la distance nous a découragés / ne nous a pas enthousiasmés, mais nous avons fini par tellement apprécier notre voyage.*

- a road – *une route*

    What's great about this village is that there are many large roads around – *Ce qui est bien avec ce village, c'est qu'il y a beaucoup de grandes routes autour.*

- a highway – *une autoroute*

    We'll probably take the highway – *Nous allons probablement prendre l'autoroute.*

- to give a ride, give a lift – *emmener en voiture, ramener en voiture*

    He gave me a ride back to the train station – *Il m'a emmenée jusqu'à la gare en voiture.* (emmenée – is the feminine if the speaker is female)

    Can you give me a lift back home? – *Peux-tu me ramener à la maison ?*

- to drive – *conduire*

    I'll drive until we reach the outskirts – *Je conduirai jusqu'à ce que nous arrivions en périphérie.*

    >>> the outskirts – *la périphérie, la zone en périphérie.*

- a path, a trail – *un chemin*

We followed a trail into the woods – *Nous avons suivi un chemin dans les bois.*

Trips and holidays:

- a trip – *un voyage, une excursion* (*excursion* is more suited for group trips or hiking sessions in rough terrain)

>My trip to the Seychelles was wonderful! – *Mon voyage aux Seychelles était génial !*

>I won't forget our trip to the top of the mountain – *Je n'oublierai pas notre voyage / notre excursion jusqu'au sommet de la montagne.*

- a holiday / holidays – *des vacances* (always plural)

- to get / go on / take holidays – *obtenir des vacances / aller en vacances / prendre des vacances*

>I have got holidays in February; I'll probably go and visit Scotland – *J'ai obtenu des vacances en février ; j'irai probablement visiter l'Ecosse.*

>We'll go on holidays in a small Greek village – *Nous irons en vacances dans un petit village grec.*

- abroad – *à l'étranger*

- to visit (a place) – *visiter un endroit*

>We visited an ancient castle at night – *Nous avons visité un château très vieux de nuit.*

- to visit (someone) – *rendre visite à quelqu'un*

>He asked us to visit him when we'd have the time – *Il nous a demandé de lui rendre visite quand nous en aurions le temps.*

- to stay (in an accommodation) – *être, rester, séjourner*

According to this leaflet, we'll stay in a local apartment for two days – *Selon ce prospectus, nous serons / resterons / séjournerons dans un appartement local pour deux jours.*

>>> a leaflet – *un prospectus.*

>>> for two days / weeks / months – *pour deux jours / semaines / mois.*

- to unplug (get away from technology) – *se déconnecter*

I'll finally get to unplug for a while – *Je pourrai enfin me déconnecter pour un temps.*

>>> for a while – *pour un temps, pendant un temps, pendant quelques temps* (all similar).

- time off – *des congés* (if granted by your employer), *du temps libre* (allocated by yourself / your employer)

I've got to take some time off – *Il faut que je prenne des congés / du temps libre.*

- free time – *du temps libre, du temps de libre*

I was given some free time, so I decided to come visit you! – *On m'a donné un peu de temps libre, donc j'ai décidé de venir te rendre visite !*

- a break (from work) – *une pause, un arrêt*

I should take advantage of my two-week break and get a change of scenery – *Je devrais profiter de ma pause de deux semaines et changer d'air.*

>>> to take advantage of – *profiter de.*

>>> get a change of scenery – *changer d'air.*

- at the beach, in the countryside, in the mountains – *à la plage / mer, à la campagne, à la montagne*

> I'm going to the beach this summer: that'll be a breath of fresh air! – *Je vais à la plage cet été : ça sera une bouffée d'air frais !*
>
> >>> a breath of fresh air – *une bouffée d'air frais.*

- in a new country / in new surroundings – *dans un nouveau pays / dans un nouveau cadre, dans un nouvel environnement* (*cadre* and *environnement,* although they translate a plural word here, will stay in the singular)

> It'll spice things up a bit, to find myself in new surroundings – *ça ajoutera un peu de piquant, de me retrouver dans un nouvel environnement.*

- the unknown – *l'inconnu*

> Let's dive into the unknown! – *Plongeons dans l'inconnu !*

Things to do:

- a guide (person) – *un guide, guide de voyages*

- a guide book – *un guide, guide de voyages*

- a tourist attraction – *une attraction touristique*

- a gourmet market – *un marché gourmand*

- a local meetup – *une rencontre locale, une réunion locale (un meetup* is also accepted because of the website Meetup.com, which is used in France*)*

- a tourist trap – *un attrape touristes*

- a hotel – *un hôtel*

- a hostel – *une auberge* (youth hostel: *auberge de jeunesse*)

- a bed and breakfast – *une chambre d'hôtes, un gîte* ; more rarely, *un bed and breakfast*

> We discovered many beautiful regions of France while we were staying in this bed and breakfast – *Nous avons*

découvert beaucoup de belles régions de France pendant que nous étions dans son gîte.

- a seaside resort – *une station balnéaire*

- a campsite - *un camping*

- a motorhome stopover / parking – *une aire d'arrêt pour camping-cars / un parking pour camping-cars*

- to rent (a car, a place to sleep) – *louer (une voiture, un endroit où dormir)*

- a rent – *un loyer*

- a deposit – *une caution*

You'll have to pay a deposit right away – *Il vous faudra payer une caution tout de suite.*

Nature and Landscapes:

- a castle – *un château*

- an inn – *une auberge*

- a medieval village – *un village médiéval*

- a village – *un village*

- a borough – *un quartier*

- a neighborhood – *un quartier*

- a park – *un parc*

- a forest – *une forêt*

- a tree – *un arbre*

- a clearing – *une clairière*

- a lagoon – *un lagon*

- a lake – *un lac*

- a river – *une rivière*

- the sea – *la mer*

- the coast – *la côte*

> We went to the coast for a couple of days – *Nous sommes allés sur la côte pour quelques jours.*

- a beach – *une plage*

> I particularly enjoy strolling along the beach – *J'aime particulièrement me balader tranquillement le long de la plage.*
>
> \>>> to stroll along – *se balader tranquillement.*

- a shore – *un rivage*

- a cliff – *une falaise*

- a mountain – *une montagne*

- a valley – *une vallée*

- a chasm – *un gouffre, un fossé*

- unwelcoming – *inhospitalier*

> I found that place rather unwelcoming – *J'ai trouvé cet endroit plutôt inhospitalier.*

Conclusion

We do hope you found this book useful in boosting your oral and written expression in French. It is undoubtedly a very rewarding language to learn, and having the possibility to dig a little deeper will strengthen your confidence and enable you to make even bigger leaps. Given how so much revolves around actions and verbs in our daily lives, we hope the "verb bank" will have given you enough insight into French's most common verbs to describe the world around you or talk about what you like doing, to help you expand your vocabulary. We particularly encourage you to start making flashcards or simply apply this new knowledge right now to retain it more easily.

Now that you have a broader view of how to describe everything from where you are – be it on holidays or in a house – to people and items, and talk about common actions, you're on the way to seeing the world in French. Even if it's just a matter of adding a word here and there or not quite remembering a word, but still knowing that you've learnt it, you'll improve your French in no time! Your vocabulary and comprehension will thus increase over time and you'll soon find yourself able to dig even deeper into the nuances and specificities of the French language.

We would also like to reemphasize that creating word lists and vocabulary banks is a very powerful way to learn new vocabulary: not only can you note down words with the same root, but also add synonyms or antonyms for a quick review and to cultivate richer expressions. We hope you have caught the "list-bug" as well, and that you create your own to review whenever and wherever you can. Using the tips from this book as your first step, you will soon be speaking like a local. Au revoir!

Check out another book by Simple Language Learning

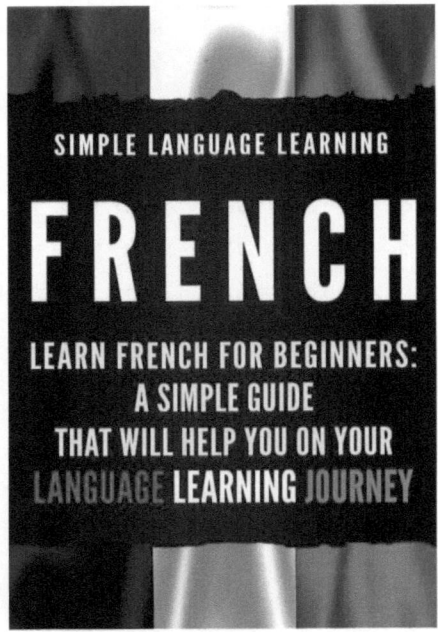

www.ingramcontent.com/pod-product-compliance
Lightning Source LLC
Chambersburg PA
CBHW030119100526
44591CB00009B/451